DOG ENRICHMENT

Family-friendly Games and Activities for You and Your Dog

Dr Anna Muir

THE CROWOOD PRESS

DOG
ENRICHMENT

Family-friendly Games and
Activities for You and Your Dog

CONTENTS

INTRODUCTION:
What Is Enrichment?

Meeting Our Dog's Needs

Our dogs are valued members of our family and are no longer faced with the daily challenges of finding enough food to eat, keeping safe from threats and finding shelter in order to survive. We meet all their basic needs by providing them with food and water, sharing our warm and cosy houses with them, taking them to the vets when they are unwell and making sure no scary predators can come and hurt them. Job done? Well, not completely, because we want our dogs not just to survive but to thrive. We want them to find fulfilment in their existence and that means meeting their higher needs of social connection and mental challenge through choice, novelty and problem-solving with their family – whether those family members have two legs or four. That is what enrichment is, making sure that all of your dog's needs are met: physical, mental and emotional. By meeting our dog's needs, we are creating happy dogs and, seeing as they bring us so much happiness, it seems like a fair exchange.

Enrichment for Captive Animals

Great, we understand the concept of enrichment. We're on board and keen to get started. How do we go about doing it? How do we know the needs of our dogs? How do we ensure that the activities we plan will meet those needs? To answer these questions, it is useful to look at where the concept of enrichment originally started: in zoos.

Have you ever been to a zoo and noticed how zookeepers feed the animals? The tigers aren't given their meat in a silver bowl; the monkeys don't sit nicely around a table. Their food is scattered, hidden and placed just out of reach. The tigers have to climb a high pole to retrieve their dinner and the monkeys have to get their fruit out of the inside of logs. Why? Because it provides a mental and physical challenge, which occupies the animals and fulfils their day-to-day life.

Zoos once contained small, barren, concrete cages inhabited by some very sad-looking animals indeed. The classic images of the repetitively pacing bear and the motionless and silent chimpanzee

▲ Our dogs bring us so much joy and they deserve a life filled with joy in return.

are examples of unhappy animals that are chronically stressed and under-stimulated. It wasn't until the 1960s that people began to consider how these animals compared with their active and engaged wild counterparts. As research into the behaviour of wild animals progressed, scientists were able to uncover what different species did when in the wild and to start setting up enclosures to make it possible for captive animals to do the same. For instance, meerkats live in groups, spend a lot of time digging, sleep and hide underground, and always have a lookout posted on higher ground to keep watch for predators. Now zoos have mobs of meerkats living together, provide them with sandy substrate to dig in, create sleeping areas that mimic underground burrows, and have high places like fake termite mounds and upturned tree trunks for meerkats on sentry duty. The animal welfare movement was born, and captive animals now live mentally and physically healthier, longer lives, with better reproductive success. In other words, they are happier.

Canine Enrichment

Now let's apply these concepts to our dogs. 'How do they behave in the wild?' is a difficult question when it comes to domesticated animals. Let's rule out the idea of wolves as wild versions of dogs. With around 15,000 years of natural and artificial selection, including physiological, morphological and behavioural changes, between them and our current dogs, the comparison isn't accurate. Current scientific evidence points to genetic changes including an increase in boldness around humans, which allowed a move from wild hunting in a pack to scavenging on waste from human habitations at a very early stage in their domestication process. The idea of dogs as pack animals, always trying to be alpha of their hunting group, is completely outdated and scientifically disproven (see Chapter 8 for more details).

The closest we've got to wild dogs currently in

▲ Helping our dogs experience different sights, sounds, smells, textures and tastes is key to enriching their lives.

existence are 'street' or 'free-living' dogs that exist within the human urban environment but are not under human management. They are seen in many locations around the world and are prevalent in India, Russia and South America. These dogs are scavengers, feeding off human rubbish and taking shelter wherever they can find it in the urban landscape. This includes, famously, using the underground train stations of Russia as a place of warmth in the winter. Dogs roam the streets, exploring the sights, sounds and smells of their environment and searching for food to scavenge, in between finding comfortable spots for a nap. This gives us a major clue as to how our dogs would spend their lives if they had choice and freedom. Investigating sights, sounds, smells, textures and tastes, and choosing which activities to do and when, is a key part of enrichment for your dog.

Breed-Specific Enrichment

We can look further into what our dog might enjoy by starting to think about what breed (or mix of breeds) they are. As humans, we are always tinkering with the genetic make-up of domesticated animals, to promote the characteristics that are useful for our day-to-day life. Predominantly, we have done this through breeding animals that possess traits that are desirable at the time, such as the ability to run fast, to be a certain size, or to have a good sense of smell. By breeding together individuals that show these traits, we hope that they will be inherited by their offspring. Due to the natural variability in how traits are inherited and expressed, we can further select which animals to breed together from those offspring, so that over time the trait becomes more and more exaggerated. For instance, if I wanted to create smaller dogs, I would systematically breed the smallest dogs from successive litters together (of different lineages preferably, although this hasn't always been the case in modern breeding practices). This would mean that over multiple generations, the genes for smallness would be inherited, until I was left with a very small dog indeed. This is the basis of how all the different breeds of dogs that we see today have been created.

This process of selective breeding by humans has led us to the extremes of body shape and temperament that we see today: from the Chihuahua to the Great Dane, from the French Bulldog to the Springer Spaniel. Each of the breeds that exist today have been bred over multiple generations for a specific purpose and are generally classified us-

▲ Herding breeds have been bred to watch, stalk and chase and have a genetic predisposition to show these behaviours even in the absence of livestock.

ing seven groups: gundog, hound, pastoral, terrier, toy, utility and working. To understand how these groups and breeds differ, we need to understand their predatory motor pattern (PMP). The PMP is the full sequence of behaviours from spotting prey, through stalking and chasing, to grabbing and killing, then eating the prey during a hunt.

To create dogs that were useful to us for specific purposes, we enhanced or supressed different parts of their PMP through breeding. For instance, to enable Labrador Retrievers to bring back things that we had killed, the orient (spotting prey) and

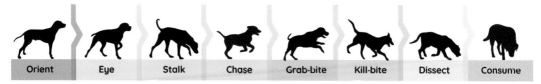

| Orient | Eye | Stalk | Chase | Grab-bite | Kill-bite | Dissect | Consume |

▲ The PMP includes all the behaviours a dog would show while hunting, catching and consuming prey. Different breeds have been bred to carry out different parts of this sequence.

grab-bite instincts had to be strong but the kill-bite and dissect elements had to be weak. For Terriers to hunt vermin as pest control, the chase, grab-bite and kill-bite instincts had to be exaggerated. For Bernese Mountain Dogs, as livestock guarders, all parts of the PMP had to be suppressed, while Border Collies needed strong orient, eye, stalk and chase instincts but weak grab-bite and kill-bite instincts. The areas of the PMP that have been exaggerated through breeding are really fun for dogs to carry out and they will get a rush of happy hormones every time they do it. Having a look at the background to your specific dog's breed will therefore help you learn what they have a tendency to enjoy. You can then build this into your enrichment plan. If you have a lovely crossbreed, then have a look at all the background breeds. If you're not sure of any of the breeds that make up your dog, don't worry – even within a breed, every individual is different so you can just try lots of different activities and see which your dog enjoys!

Enrichment for Your Dog

Are these dog- and breed-specific behaviours starting to sound familiar? Has your pup ever scavenged something disgusting and eaten it while out on a walk? Dug up your lawn? Carried your favourite shoes around? Tried to round up your visitors? Well, guess what – our dogs will always find ways of fulfilling their needs one way or another. We can't suppress their natural behaviours; they will always find an outlet for them, whether we approve of it or not! Telling them off for expressing their genetically predetermined behaviours, many of which we have bred them to do, seems pretty unreasonable, doesn't it? So how about we provide them with enrichment outlets for these behaviours that are acceptable to us humans and satisfying for our dogs? Let's work with our dogs rather than against them. Every dog is different and your role is to ensure that the enrichment that you are offering is right for your specific dog. It isn't en-

▲ All dogs are individuals, even within the same breed, so find out what your dog enjoys the most by trying different activities with them.

richment if your dog isn't motivated to participate or is forced to join in when they don't want to. In order to work with your dog to enrich their lives, play around with difficulty level, support motivation and ensure that they have choice.

Difficulty Level

Set up your enrichment games and activities at a difficulty level that is challenging but doable for your dog. No one enjoys a game where they never win! If they aren't used to using their noses to find food, make the food easy to find at first. If you are scatter feeding (see Chapter 1), pour their food on the grass in a pile the first time then gradually spread it in larger and larger areas around the garden. If you are hiding a toy for them to find (see Chapter 1), start by placing the toy right in the middle of the room, then to one side of the room, before gradually progressing to hiding it behind sofas and under cushions. Feel free to help your dog by pointing to the toy and excitedly encouraging them to find it – you're a team after all. The more that

Each breed is predisposed to like certain types of activities, but don't forget that your dog is also an individual and may vary from these guidelines.

Group	Purpose bred for	Example breeds	Tends to enjoy
Gundog	To find and retrieve game	Cocker Spaniel, Labrador, Golden Retriever, German Wire-haired Pointer and Irish Setter	Following scent trails, chasing and holding items
Hound	To search for and chase game	Greyhound, Whippet Beagle, Dachshund and Basset Hound	Following scent trails (scent hounds) and chasing moving items (sight hounds)
Pastoral	To herd livestock	Border Collie, German Shepherd, Belgian Malinois, Welsh Corgi and Australian cattle dog	Stalking and grouping items
Terrier	To kill vermin	Jack Russell Terrier, Border Terrier, Staffordshire Bull Terrier and Bedlington Terrier	Chasing, digging, grabbing items and pulling items apart
Toy	As a human companion	Chihuahua, Yorkshire Terrier, Shih Tzu, Italian Greyhound and Maltese	Activities that focus on human interaction
Utility	A variety of purposes that don't fall within the other groupings	Bulldog, Dalmation, Poodle, Akita and Miniature Schnauzer	Each breed has a separate purpose in this group so will need to be researched separately, e.g. bulldogs tend to enjoy grabbing and tugging items
Working	To guard or for search and rescue	Siberian Husky, Boxer Bernese Mountain Dog, Rottweiler, Doberman, and Newfoundland	Independent, problem-solving activities

you join in with the hunt, the more they will enjoy it. I've heard owners say, 'My dog has a rubbish nose, they can't find anything', but the truth is, using scent to find objects is a skill that needs practice, just like learning to ride a bike or play the guitar. If you set up activities so that they are too hard for your dog, for example wrapping treats in too many layers of toilet roll and paper to begin with for the pup puzzle box (see Chapter 2), then they will soon become demotivated and stop trying. If your dog isn't interested in the activity or game, have a think about how you can make it easier for them to begin with.

◀ If your dog is new to enrichment, as all puppies are, start with simple tasks and help them to be successful. This will increase their motivation and confidence to try harder activities in the future.

REWARD CHOICE GAME

1 Choose five different food rewards that you think your dog might like. This could be from a bag of treats from the shop, one of the recipes in Chapter 4, something you have in the kitchen like cheese, cooked meat, berries or apple or your dog's own food. Take a small piece of each of the treats and place them in a row on the floor.

2 Allow your dog to enter the room and watch which treat they eat first, which treats they also choose to eat, and which treats (if any) they leave on the floor.

3 You've now discovered which treats your dog likes and which is their favourite.

4 Choose five different types of toys, such as a tennis ball, a plastic bone, a tug rope and different stuffed toys. Line them up on the floor as before.

5 Allow your dog to enter the room and watch which toys they show interest in. Also pay attention to how they play with them. Do they run around holding the toy in their mouth? Do they drop the toy for you to throw? Do they enjoy a game of tug?

6 You've now identified their favourite toys and how you might play with them with those toys to maximise their enjoyment.

Now that you know your dog's favourite things, you can use these to motivate them to engage with enrichment. Try this game at different times of day and see if your dog makes the same choices, as their favourite may vary depending on whether they are full or hungry, tired or have just had a nap. Plus, remember that dogs love novelty so rotate their favourite things within the activities to keep them interested!

Motivation

The second key element is motivation. Is the reward interesting enough to your dog for them to work to access it? If they don't want whatever you've hidden then they won't try to find it. If they don't like the reward then they won't work hard through training to receive it. Start thinking about what your dog loves to do and enjoys to eat and include these things in your enrichment activities. For instance, does your dog prefer toys or treats?

What is their favourite toy? How do they like to play with it? What is their favourite food? Try out the reward choice game to help you find out.

Choice

Finally, the most important point: it is crucial that you allow your dog to choose whether they want to take part in an activity. Dogs need to feel safe to engage in play and enrichment. What makes

▲ Find out what your dog enjoys the most and use those items as rewards for games, activities and training.

▲ Have fun with your dog through enrichment activities and you'll find that all your lives are enriched.

them feel safe? Choice. They need to be able to opt in and opt out of scenarios depending on how they feel about them. There is a recent craze for escape rooms. You are placed in a room and have to solve puzzles to free yourself. When you have chosen to join in this game: fun. Locked in a room against your will and desperately trying to find ways to get out: not fun. In the first scenario, you know that you have opted in to take part and that in actuality you can leave at any time, so you feel safe and you can enjoy yourself. Your dog needs to have the same option. Give them the option to walk away from the game or stop the activity at any point and they will feel much more comfortable to join in when they are ready. Does your dog look uncomfortable, are they trying to move away, have they stopped taking rewards? Listen to them. Let them take a break and come back to it when they are ready. They will trust you all the more for it.

How to Use This Book

This book is a guide to activities that you can do with and for your dog. All activities are designed to be simple and accessible so that all members of your family, whether they have two legs or four, can find activities they can do and get involved with. This book will enrich your life as well as that of your dog! As with all new activities, en-sure that your dog gets a full vet check prior to starting the enrichment in this book, to make sure that they don't have any physical limitations or hidden pain that could affect which activities are most suitable for your dog at this time.

The first part of this book gives detailed descriptions of the activities, including games, crafts, movement, baking and tricks. This part is designed to be browsed and dipped in and out of as you choose an activity you would like to do with your dog. In the Appendix there is a tick list that you can tick off when you have tried each activity. The second part of the book details when and how you can use the activities to enrich the life of your dog. Here you will find specific information about how and when to use enrichment, including meeting your dog's needs when they are puppies, overexcited teenagers, on walks, when they can't go on walks, when your family includes children, through training and to promote health in dogs with physical and behavioural limitations. You can choose the chapters that are most applicable to you and your dog as you go through life. The enrichment plans in the final chapter will aid you in choosing the enrichment activities most suitable for your situation.

Above all, this book is about creating happy dogs and happy families, and I hope you and your dog find lots of ways to have fun together within its pages.

CHAPTER ONE:
Games

The games included here focus on using your dog's natural tendencies to search, find, grab, hold and consume. There are some games that take seconds to set up and some that require more effort. All of them can be increased or decreased in difficulty to give your dog an achievable challenge. Many of them involve using food rewards – remember that these can be small pieces, just to give your dog a taste of the good stuff; there is no need to give them a huge chunk every time. Good options include small training treats (try the recipes in Chapter 4), blueberries, chopped-up apple or carrots, small pieces of plain cooked meat, cheese or pâté or a lick of dog-friendly peanut butter. Why not take your dog's usual breakfast and dinner and instead of serving it in a bowl, give it to them using one of the games?

Treasure Hunt

This treasure hunt will put your dog's nose to work as they follow a trail of treats. They won't have a treasure map to guide them, but they will have their excellent sense of smell, which will lead them from one treat to the next. At the end of the trail, they will find their very own treasure. Even if your dog is not very practised at using their nose (perhaps they can't find a treat even when you drop it at their feet), start with the trail treats close together and they will soon get the idea. Before long, you will be able spread the treats further apart as your dog taps into their impressive sense of smell.

You will need:

▶ lots of small treats

▶ some treasure that your dog loves.

1. Lay a trail of treats around the room or garden.

2. End the trail behind an item of furniture or a tree so it is hidden out of sight.

3. At the end of the trail, place some treasure for your dog. This could be a bonus pile of treats, a chew, a ball or your dog's favourite toy.

4. Release your dog at the start of the trail and let them follow the treats all the way to their treasure! If they lose their way, help them by pointing out where the next treat is.

5. When they come to the end of the trail, tell them how clever they are and let them eat or play with their treasure.

6. With practice, you can increase the distance between treats and the length of the trail so that your dog goes on a merry hunt around your home and garden to find the treasure.

▲ Lay a trail of treats around your home and place a special toy or food treasure at the end of the trail for your dog to find.

Scatter Feeding

We eat from bowls so dogs should eat from bowls, right? Wrong! Dogs evolved to live with humans by scavenging on their leftovers, so they are well equipped to search out the food that they are going to eat. Add some interest to your dog's mealtimes with this simple and cost-effective game that allows your dog to use their innate abilities and keeps them entertained for much longer than food tipped in a bowl. Low effort for you and high enjoyment for your dog, it's a win-win.

▲ Scatter feeding is a simple yet effective way of adding interest to your dog's mealtimes.

You will need:

► your dog's normal food
► access to a grass area.

1. Take your dog's meal and scatter it over a patch of short grass.
2. Watch them snuffle around, searching for, and eating, their dinner.
3. As they get better at searching, scatter their food over larger areas to give them more of a challenge.

★ Your dog is getting a double reward of both searching and eating. This is great for dogs who wolf down their food quickly and for dogs who don't normally find their dinner that interesting.

★ On rainy days, you can hide their dinner in their snuffle mat or pup puzzle box (see Chapter 2) instead.

Cup Magic Trick

Have you ever seen a magician lay out three cups, put a ball under one cup, then use sleight of hand to move the cups until you aren't able identify which cup contains the ball? It's surprisingly hard to keep track of where the cup with the ball is. Well, don't worry, because now you can use your dog's nose as your magic wand. In this trick, your dog will smell which cup contains the treat and their reward is getting to eat it.

You will need:

▶ three plastic cups, bowls or plant pots

▶ a flat surface

▶ smelly treats.

▲ Your dog has a seemingly magical smelling ability and they can tell where a treat is even if they can't see it.

1. Take one plastic cup, turn it upside down and place a treat on top of it. Point to the treat and say 'Find it' as you allow your dog to eat it. Repeat this about five times, so that your dog starts to associate the cup with treats. If your dog has a habit of picking up the cup and running off with it, pick up the cup as soon as they have eaten the treat.

2. Throw a treat away to the side to distract your dog or ask your dog to 'Stay' (see Chapter 5 for how to train this cue) while you set up the next step.

3. Place the treat underneath the upturned cup. Say 'Find it' to your dog and tilt the cup so that they can get the treat from underneath. Repeat around five times so that your dog now understands that there is a treat underneath the cup when you say 'Find it'.

4. Repeat the previous step by placing a treat under the cup and cueing 'Find it', but as your dog gets the treat from under the cup, allow the cup to fall sideways onto the floor so that they get used to the sound of the cup being knocked over. Repeat five times.

5. Place the treat under the cup, cue 'Find it', but let your dog snuffle around the cup and see if they can knock it over themselves to get to the treat. Repeat five times.

6. Now you can add in a second upside-down cup next to the first but only place a treat under one of them so that your dog has to sniff each cup to work out which has the treat underneath.

7. When your dog is happily finding the treat, add in a third cup but still only place a treat under one of them. You are increasing the difficulty level for your dog as they learn this new skill.

8. Finally, after you have placed a treat under one of the cups, you can move the cups around on the floor while saying the magic words, 'Where it goes, nobody knows, but my dog's nose!'

Hide and Seek

If there is one thing that your dog loves as much as treats and toys, it's you! In this game, you are tapping into their desire to be with you by hiding out of sight and encouraging them to track you down using sight and smell. Hanging out with you should always be super fun for your dog so shower them with affection when their search and rescue mission is successful. Play this game in your garden or out on a walk – it will make sure your dog pays attention to where you are at all times. Hide and seek can be on or off lead, depending on where you are and if it's safe for your dog to be roaming free.

You will need:

- ▶ at least two people
- ▶ a location where you can hide from your dog.

▲ You can build engagement with your dog by playing hide and seek. They will be keen to keep an eye on you and will enjoy using their senses to find you.

1. One person stays with the dog and counts to twenty while the other person hides.

2. Release the dog and say 'Where are they?'

3. The dog runs around trying to track down the hiding person and is rewarded with lots of praise when they find them. If your dog is struggling to find the person hiding, a quick shout of the dog's name from the hiding place should help them track the person down.

4. When out on a walk, duck behind a tree from time to time and call your dog's name to play a shorter version of this game.

Note: If your dog gets upset when they can't see you then this is not the game for them.

Find It

Did you know that dogs enjoy the search for food as much as the eating of it? Looking for food using sight, sound and smell, and tracking it down, causes them to release dopamine – a happy hormone that makes them feel great. Even if it takes a long time to find the food, they will still carry on searching for it because that's part of the fun. When they do find food and consume it, they then release endorphins, which leaves them feeling calm and content. Hide your dog's food and you are doubling their fun.

You will need:

► treats/a stuffed food toy/a chew/a lick mat.

1. Take the food and place it just outside a door.

2. Say 'Find it', open the door and let your dog have the food. Here you are teaching them that 'Find it' means that there is food to find.

3. Repeat the first two steps, but this time place the food further away from the door to increase the challenge.

4. Next, place the food behind a plant pot, bush or tree (if in the garden) or behind a table or chair (if inside) and ask your dog to 'Find it'. Be sure to help them to find it if they are struggling.

5. Once your pup is good at finding the food, continue to increase the difficulty level by hiding it in harder-to-find places, such as behind a cushion, under a bush or on a garden seat.

6. If you stuff a toy or spread a lick mat with your dog's usual food, you can do this every mealtime.

▲ Searching for food is as enjoyable as eating it for your dog so hiding a food-stuffed toy and getting them to hunt for their dinner is double the fun.

Tree Snuffle

Enrichment doesn't have to take place just in your home; engaging with your dog while out on a walk is key to building communication between you. If your dog is paying attention to you, they are much more likely to respond when you call – especially if sometimes you call them to play a fun game. This game lets you and your dog hunt as a team to find prey (treats) hidden in the bark of a tree trunk.

You will need:

▶ soft treats, such as small chunks of cheese, pâté, hotdog sausage or sweet potato pancakes (see Chapter 4 for the recipe)

▶ access to a tree.

1. Hide some treats in cracks in the bark near the base of the tree and around the roots of the tree.

2. Call your dog and excitedly ask 'Find it' while guiding them to the tree.

▲ Hiding treats in the bark of a tree means your dog has to lift their nose off the ground to sniff, which adds an extra challenge.

3. Let them snuffle all around the base of the tree to find and eat the treats.

4. If they need help, give them a hand to find the treats by encouraging them and pointing out where the treats are.

★ Your dog will enjoy working with you as a team to find their treat prey. Use this to improve your dog's recall – your dog will learn that when you call, something exciting is about to happen and will be sure to race back to you in no time.

Tracking with Tech

Running around trying to find your dog using GPS technology is super fun for the children in your life. They can watch in real time where you are and manoeuvre around landmarks like trees and houses to sneak up on your hiding place. This is a low effort activity for your dog – just scatter some treats on the ground for them to snuffle up as they wait with you to be found. This is a great way for children to feel like they are playing with your dog, without too much pressure on the dog. This is particularly good for elderly dogs who may prefer to just stand around taking in the sights and smells rather than running around.

You will need:

► a GPS tag and tracker app.

1. Place the GPS tracker on your dog's collar and switch it on.

2. Designate a 'hider' who will take your dog to hide somewhere.

3. The 'trackers' will count to twenty while the hiders hide.

4. The trackers use the tracker app to locate and track down where your dog is hiding.

5. Increase the count to give the hiders more chance to hide further away if you want to make it more difficult for the trackers.

★ This game works well in larger open spaces so try it out in your local wood or country park.

▲ Tracking your dog using a GPS tag is a low-effort activity for your dog, which is great for dogs who have reduced mobility, while being a fun activity for the whole family.

Tug Station

Does your dog love a game of tug? Will they hold a rope toy in their mouth and pull and pull as if their life depended on it? Do they give it a good shake to make sure it's dead? Then you have a pup that is very motivated by the grab-and kill-bite part of hunting. This is common in Terrier and Bull breeds (although other breeds enjoy it too). This game will ensure that your dog can tug to their heart's desire, while saving your arms from being pulled out of their sockets! It is a safe way to let your dog act out their natural drive.

You will need:

- ▶ a tug rope (see Chapter 2 for how to make one)
- ▶ an old collar, belt, lead or strong piece of string
- ▶ a sturdy post.

1. Take your tug rope and feed the old collar through the plait of the tug rope or double-knot the collar around one end of the tug rope.

2. Find a sturdy post that is dug into the ground, such as a fence post, tree or washing line pole.

3. Fasten the collar tightly around the pole at the height of your dog's head.

4. Encourage your dog to come and play with the tug rope by excitedly calling them and moving the tug rope around.

5. Let them get hold of the tug rope and praise them as they tug.

6. When it's time for the game to finish, call your dog and sprinkle some treats onto the ground for them to snuffle and eat as a cool down.

Note: If your dog doesn't like other people or dogs near their toys then skip this game.

▲ Many dogs love to tug, so giving them an outlet for that behaviour will help them fulfil their natural drives.

Fastest Finder

This game is great if your dog loves their toys and carrying them around fills them with joy, which is especially true for Retrievers and Spaniels. They have to race other members of the family (those with two legs or four) to find their toy. Finding hidden toys can be quite challenging for dogs at first if it is a skill that they haven't much practised. As always, start with very easy hiding places (right in the middle of the room in plain sight) and move up from there.

You will need:

▶ a range of toys.

1. One person goes into a room or the garden and hides one toy belonging to each dog and one toy belonging to each of the other family members playing the game.

2. Say 'Ready, steady, go!' and release the searchers to hunt for their toy.

3. Can a person find their toy before the dog does? Which dog (if there are more than one) can find a toy? The winner is the player who finds their toy first!

4. Start hiding the toys in easy places then increase the difficulty as everyone becomes more practised. Your dog may need you to point to the toy to begin with – give them lots of praise when they pick it up.

★ Is your dog a genius and you've taught them the names of their toys? Hide a few different toys but ask them to find a specific toy. The same goes for the people in your family.

Practise finding toys with your dog and then turn it into a game for everyone to get involved in.

Muffin Tin Brain Game

By hiding treats under balls in your tin, you've created a puzzle that your dog has to solve to access the good stuff. It's very straightforward to set up and it lets your dog practise their problem-solving skills. Exercising their brain is just as important as exercising their body. Once your dog has become a whiz at accessing their treats, pop the tin in the freezer before you give it to them for an added challenge.

▲ The muffin tin brain game encourages your dog to problem-solve.

You will need:

► a muffin tin
► some tennis balls (lots of second-hand tennis balls are available online)
► some treats.

1. Place a treat in the base of each muffin tin hole.

2. Place a ball on top of the treat in each muffin tin hole.

3. Place the muffin tin on a non-slip surface on the floor.

4. Allow your dog to investigate the tin and work out how to access the treats. To get them started, you can lift up some of the balls, show them the treats hiding there and let them eat them.

5. Once the treats are all eaten, you can play with your dog with the balls.

★ If you don't have any tennis balls, you can use scrunched-up pieces of scrap paper instead.

CHAPTER 2:
Crafts

We live in a disposable world where everything is single use and made from unsustainable materials. Couple this with the fact that our dogs love, sooner or later, to destroy every toy that we give them, and we're soon creating a rubbish pile of plastic waste in our wake. I love giving my dogs new toys but I don't love wasting money on something that will be rapidly demolished. That's why this chapter is dedicated to making toys out of things that you already have in the house that would otherwise go to waste. What's more, if you've sourced the parts for the toys from your recycling bin and your pup then takes great pleasure in ripping and shredding them to access treats, it doesn't matter; they just go back in the recycling bin afterwards, saving you money, saving the environment, allowing your dog to have loads of fun and allowing you to have some fun crafting along the way!

Snuffle Mat

Your dog loves to use their nose. It is their primary sense and tracking down their food using scent alone is very rewarding for them. A snuffle mat consists of different layers of fabric that you can tuck treats underneath. Your dog will have to sniff out where these treats are in the folds of fabric before they get to eat them. The best thing is that you can make one using a couple of old sweatshirts or T-shirts. Once you've made it, you can reuse it to feed your dog, keep them entertained and calm them after a high-excitement play session.

You will need:

- ▶ two old sweatshirts or T-shirts (use as many different colours as you like to make it look fun)
- ▶ a pair of scissors.

1. Take the thicker of your old sweatshirts or T-shirts and cut out a square of around 30cm × 30cm (12in × 12in). It can be any size but with our dogs this worked well. This is your base fabric.

2. Start about 3cm (1in) from the top edge and snip 2cm-long (3/4in) vertical slits in a straight row along the length of your fabric, leaving about 3cm (1in) between each hole. Repeat this for a further eight rows, leaving about 3cm (1in) between rows, until your base is covered in small holes.

3. Take your second old jumper or T-shirt and cut out thirty-two strips of about 2cm (3/4in) × 20cm (8in).

4. Take a strip and thread it down through one hole of your base and then back up through the adjacent hole. Tie the strip in a double knot.

5. Repeat the threading and tying with your strips until all holes are filled.

6. Tuck little pieces of dry food or treats under your knotted strips, place the mat on the floor and let your pup snuffle out and eat the treats.

7. Remember to pick up the mat once your dog has retrieved all the treats so that they don't chew your mat!

▲ Your dog will love searching within the fabric folds of a snuffle mat for their food.

Digging Area

Digging is a natural behaviour in dogs and giving them the opportunity to enjoy digging in a specified area will save your lawn and flower beds. In my experience, this pastime is particularly popular with Golden Retrievers and many of the puppy owners that I've worked with have loved creating a fun area for their dogs to do what they do best – get messy! If you would like to give your dog the opportunity to show their natural behaviours but without the mud, just use children's sand to fill the area instead. Your dog gets to dig and you get to keep your garden looking nice. As with many training solutions, simple works best.

You will need:

- ▶ an area of outdoor space that you can dedicate to your dog
- ▶ some pieces of wood (planks, branches, sticks or whatever you have available)
- ▶ nails and a hammer (if using planks)
- ▶ string (if using branches and sticks)
- ▶ soil or children's sand.

▲ If your dog loves to dig then providing them with a 'legal' digging area will save your flower beds from 'illegal' digging.

1. Identify where you would like your digging area to be in your outdoor space. If you are using sand, an area with a hard base is best (such as a patio) as it will stop the sand mixing with mud and allow you to sweep up and return any sand that gets thrown out.

2. Create a frame for your digging area by hammering together planks or tying together branches into a rectangular shape. How big you make this rectangle depends on the space that you have and the size of your dog. For optimum digging fun, they should be able to fit the length of their body inside the frame. If you have an old hard-plastic children's paddling pool available then this is a great option too.

3. Fill your frame with soil or sand.

4. Hide treats and toys inside the digging area and encourage your pup to dig to find them – help by revealing the first few treasures for them.

5. Every time that your pup tries to dig elsewhere in your garden, call them over and encourage them to dig in their digging area instead.

6. Keep it interesting by adding more treats and toys inside the digging area from time to time. This is especially important while they are learning to use the area. In time, this will become the place that your dog heads to when they feel the urge to do some digging.

Pup Puzzle Box

A pup puzzle box is a firm favourite in our household. Whenever Christmas or our dogs' birthdays come around, my children and I love to gather up the toilet rolls we've been saving, raid the scrap paper collection and put together one of these boxes. Seeing our dogs enthusiastically delve into the box to shred and tear to reach their treats is a lot of fun to watch – if a little messy afterwards! The good news is that all the mess can just be swept up and placed in the recycling bin. This box gives your dog a fantastic opportunity to rip up and destroy something, without wrecking your slippers. It is enjoyed by all dogs but is especially good for Terriers.

You will need:

▶ a cardboard box (make sure the sides aren't too tall for your dog – they should be able to lean over and put their head in)

▶ toilet rolls

▶ scrap paper

▶ treats.

▲ The pup puzzle box involves searching for, finding and ripping apart containers to access treats, making it a very fulfilling activity for your dog.

1. Take a toilet roll and block one end by placing a scrunched-up ball of paper in it or by folding the end over.

2. Put some treats into the toilet roll.

3. Block the other end with more scrunched-up paper.

4. Repeat with as many toilet rolls as you like.

5. Tuck in or cut off the top flaps of your cardboard box.

6. Place the toilet rolls into the cardboard box.

7. Take a piece of scrap paper, put some treats in the middle, and scrunch it up to conceal the treats.

8. Repeat with as many pieces of paper as you like and place them into the cardboard box.

9. Sprinkle more treats over the paper and toilet rolls.

10. Place on the floor and invite your dog to find the treats!

★ As your dog gets better at finding the treats, you can also place a tea towel over the top of the box so that they first have to remove it to get into the box. You could add some of their favourite toys to the box too.

Crunchy Sock Toy

This easy-to-make toy is nice and soft on your pup's mouth but makes a fabulous crunching sound when they bite it. They will love chomping on it and throwing it around, and when they do, the treats will rattle, providing extra entertainment! What's more, it will allow puppies to get used to some loud noises, which can help with confidence in day-to-day life. If having the treats inside the bottle drives your dog a bit too wild in their attempt to access them, leave the bottle empty instead.

You will need:

▶ an empty plastic bottle

▶ a sock

▶ a handful of small hard treats.

1. Clean the bottle and remove and throw away the lid and label.

2. Place your treats into the bottle to give it a good rattling sound.

3. Place the bottle inside a sock and tie a knot at the top (make sure the knot is secure so that your dog can't remove it. If they do manage to, take the sock away so that there is no risk of swallowing it).

4. Give it to your dog and let them happily crunch away with their new toy!

▲ The crunchy sock toy feels great between your dog's teeth and makes a loud noise, which adds to the entertainment.

T-Shirt Tug Rope

Many dogs love to play tug of war, where you hold one end and they hold the other and you both pull. Bull breeds are particularly fond of this type of game and it is very rewarding for them as it gives them an outlet for this behaviour, rather than tugging on your clothes. If you have a large dog you can add in more strands of T-shirt to make a chunkier tug rope. Remember to let your dog win the tug of war sometimes too – nobody likes a game where they always lose! This toy is also nice to use for a game of fetch for dogs who prefer to retrieve rather than tug.

You will need:

▶ two old T-shirts in different colours

▶ scissors.

1. Cut each T-shirt up the side seams to give a front and a back piece.

2. Snip each T-shirt piece horizontally along the side hem, about every 5cm (2in).

3. Rip upwards from each snip to create strips until you have six strips of one colour (colour A) and eight strips of the other colour (colour B).

4. Place the strips on a flat surface in the following order: four of colour A, four of colour B, four of colour A.

5. Tightly knot the strips together at the top using a strip of colour B (see image right).

6. Plait the strips together in a basic three-strand plait pattern by crossing the left-hand colour A strips over the colour B strips into the middle, then the right-hand colour A strips into the middle. Repeat, taking the left-hand then right-hand strips into the middle, until you reach the end of your strips.

7. Tightly knot the strips together at the bottom using a strip of colour B.

8. Have lots of fun with your dog playing tug and fetch.

▲ The versatile tug rope can be used to play tug, fetch, wriggled along the floor for your dog to chase, and chewed on – multiple ways of having fun from just two old T-shirts.

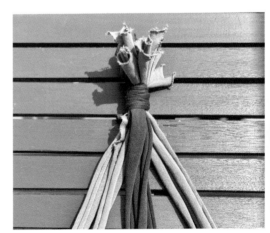

▲ Lay out three strands of strips and tie them together at the top, ready to plait your tug rope.

Flirt Pole

Many dogs love to chase small furry things whenever they get the opportunity. As running after wildlife to satisfy their need to hunt is not a good option, we can give them safe ways to express this natural behaviour. A flirt pole is like a fishing rod with a toy attached to the end that allows you to move the toy around as if it is running away from your dog. They can then stalk, chase and pounce to try to catch it. This game is especially enjoyable for Terriers, who have an innate desire to catch small animals, having been bred to control vermin. Don't forget to let your pup catch their quarry from time to time!

You will need:

- ▶ a long stick, such as a garden cane or a small branch from a tree
- ▶ 1m (3ft) of elastic (you can use string here but stretchy elastic is safer for your dog as it buffers against sudden jolts when they catch hold of the prey)
- ▶ duct or parcel tape
- ▶ a soft toy or tug rope (see the T-shirt tug rope activity for how to make one).

1. Take your length of elastic and tie one end firmly to the end of your stick.

2. Wrap tape around the knotted end to hold it in place on your stick. This is especially useful if using a slippery garden cane.

3. Tie your dog's toy firmly to the other end of the elastic.

4. Start by slowly wiggling the toy along the floor to get your dog's attention.

5. When they start to chase it, rapidly move the toy along the floor so that they have to run after it.

6. Allow your dog to pounce and catch the toy.

7. When their grip on the toy loosens, rapidly move the toy away again to repeat the chase and pounce.

8. At the end of the game, sprinkle some treats on the floor for your dog to search for and eat to calm their excitement levels while you put the flirt pole away.

▲ Moving toys are so much more fun than stationary ones. Get your pup chasing and catching using a flirt pole.

Egg Box Rolls

For this activity, your dog pulls out and unrolls treat-filled fabric strips from inside an egg box. This activity has quite a high level of difficulty for your dog and even took my own enrichment ninja longer than usual. It's a nice option if your dog finishes most food puzzles in seconds!

If your dog is new to enrichment, a nice first activity is to place treats inside the egg box without the fabric. You can then progress to using the fabric rolls when your dog understands the concept and knows that tasty things hide in egg boxes.

You will need:

▶ an empty egg box

▶ an old T-shirt or tea towel

▶ hard dog treats

▶ scissors.

▲ Egg box rolls are an advanced activity that requires skill and focus for your dog to access the hidden treats.

1. Turn your egg box upside down and cut off the flat base of each egg holder.

2. Take your old T-shirt and cut it into six strips of approximately 5cm (2in) × 25cm (10in); if using a thicker material like a tea towel, the strips may need to be shorter to fit in the egg box.

3. Take one of your fabric strips. Place some treats at the short end of the strip and roll lengthways, adding a few extra treats after every few rolls, until you have a fabric roll with treats inside.

4. Place the roll into one of the holes that you made in the egg box with just the tip of it poking out.

5. Repeat with the other five pieces of fabric.

6. Place down on the floor and encourage your dog to find the treats hidden within.

Finn's Doggy Bag

My eldest son, Finn, was seven when he created, trialled and wrote up the instructions for this doggy bag. He made it for our dog when she was recovering from an operation and couldn't do any physical activity. It allowed her to rip up the paper bag and then snuffle around in the shredded paper for the treats, keeping her excellently entertained. Now he would like to share this activity with you and he hopes your dog enjoys it as much as ours did.

You will need:

▶ two pieces of paper
▶ a handful of hard dog treats
▶ sticky tape.

1. Take a piece of paper, fold it in half and tape along two sides to make a bag with an open end.

2. Take your other piece of paper and rip it into small strips.

3. Place the shredded paper and the treats into your paper bag.

4. Fold over the open side of your bag and give your envelope a good shake to mix the treats and shredded paper.

5. Give it to your dog and allow them to tear open the bag and search through the shredded paper to pick out the treats hiding inside.

6. Once the treats have all been eaten, remove the paper so that your dog doesn't decide to snack on that too.

▲ Ripping, shredding and eating treats is lots of fun for your dog.

Spin the Bottle

With this advanced game, your dog has to knock a bottle suspended on a string into an upside-down position so that treats fall out onto the ground. They can do this using their mouth, nose or paws to find the technique that works best for them. To avoid frustration, give your dog a hand to begin with until they work out an effective technique.

You will need:

- ▶ an empty plastic bottle
- ▶ string
- ▶ scissors
- ▶ a table that is taller than your dog
- ▶ a marker pen
- ▶ small, hard treats.

▲ Your dog has to spin the bottle upside down to get the treats to fall out so they can eat them.

1. Take the lid and wrapper off your bottle and throw them away.

2. Stand your bottle upright and mark two points directly opposite each other, halfway up your bottle.

3. Use your scissors to cut small holes at each of the marks.

4. Pass your length of string through these holes.

5. Tie either end of the string to adjacent table legs at about the height of your dog's head. You should end up with the bottle suspended on the string under the edge of your table.

6. Hold the bottle upright and fill with small, hard treats.

7. Show your dog how, when the bottle spins, treats fall out.

8. Let them work out how to spin the bottle to access the treats.

★ This activity can take a while for a dog to figure out so make sure the treats inside are really good to keep them motivated and that you help them as needed.

Tea Towel Challenge

This is a lovely introductory activity for puppies, as you can start easy and move through the levels as your dog becomes a more accomplished problem-solver. If your puppy is teething (teething peaks at around four to six months old) then you can also put the tea towel in the freezer for a while prior to giving it to them, to soothe their gums. Expect some holes in your tea towels but keep an eye that your dog isn't actually swallowing any of the fabric.

You will need:

▶ a tea towel
▶ hard treats.

Easy

1. Take a tea towel and spread some treats all over the top of it.
2. Point to the treats and allow your dog snuffle and eat them off the towel.

Medium

1. Take a tea towel and spread some treats all over the top of it.
2. Fold the corners of the tea towel into the middle to hide the treats under the folds.
3. Encourage your dog to search under the fabric to find the treats.

Hard

1. Take a tea towel and spread some treats all over the top of it.
2. Roll the tea towel up into a long sausage.
3. Place it on the floor and call your dog over.
4. Start to unroll it slowly so that the first few treats are exposed and allow your dog to eat them.

5. Leave your dog to sniff at the tea towel and work out how to unroll it to access all the other treats. Make sure that the treats are evenly spread across the tea towel so that they access treats frequently as they unroll it, which will motivate them to keep working at the puzzle.

★ Has your dog worked out that they can grab the corner of the towel, pull, and all the treats fall out, making it super easy for them to eat them? Well done, your dog is a problem-solving genius – move on to the next level!

Advanced

1. Take a tea towel and spread some treats all over the top of it.
2. Roll the tea towel up into a long sausage.
3. Loosely knot the towel.
4. Watch your dog's brain work as they try to figure out how to access the treats.

▲ With four levels of difficulty to the tea towel challenge game, you can find the perfect difficulty level for your dog and then progress as your dog practises their skills.

CHAPTER 3:
Movement

Mental enrichment and physical enrichment go hand in hand when considering our dogs' wellbeing. Daily walks can be wonderful experiences for dogs and owners alike but it is not the only way for your dog to enjoy moving their body. Indeed, ensuring that your dog builds their muscles, maintains core strength and improves their balance can require forms of movement other than just walking. Working with your dog so that they experience different types of movement, whether that's weaving between poles or balancing on a plank, allows them to gain greater understanding of how to move their bodies, which leads to greater confidence when standing on the vet's table or travelling in a moving car. Ensuring that your dog is healthy and has full functional movement will reduce the risk of injury and keep them active into old age, which can extend their life. There are also times in our dogs' lives when walks might not be appropriate: maybe your dog is stressed by things that they see outside, it's too hot to go out or you aren't physically able to walk them. For these and other instances, it is great to have a bank of physical activities that you can use with your pup.

Barking Burpees

These dog burpees follow a repeated Sit-Down-Stand pattern and are great for leg strength and mobility, maintaining joint movement and core stability. They can be challenging for older dogs or those with joint conditions so keep the pace nice and slow so that they can mindfully move their bodies between each of the stages. If your dog shows any hesitation with any of the moves, then skip this activity or modify it for them. For instance, my dog with osteoarthritis in her hips is happy doing a repeated Down-Stand pattern but is less willing to do a Sit, so we skip this step. If your dog has a health condition, always check with your vet before trying an activity.

> ### You will need:
>
> ▶ your dog to know the cues Sit, Down and Stand (see Chapter 5 for how to train these).

1. Cue your dog to Sit, hold for one second, reward.

2. Cue your dog to Down, hold for one second, reward.

3. Cue your dog to Stand, hold for one second, reward.

4. Repeats steps 1–3, gradually increasing how long they hold the position, a second at a time, from one to five seconds.

5. Repeat the Sit-Down-Stand sequence.

6. As your dog learns the moves, you can run through the whole sequence before each reward.

▲ Slow, repetitive movements help your dog build strength.

Balance Trail

A balance trail is a walkway laid out on your floor consisting of varied non-slip surfaces that encourage your dog to focus on their body positioning. It is great for pets recovering from neurological injury, and for puppies as part of their sensory development and to improve their balance. It's a fun activity to get children involved in as they will enjoy setting up and following the trail too.

You will need:

▶ a selection of items that can be placed on the floor and stood on by your dog, such as rugs, mats, planks of wood, cushions, bubble wrap, a low gym step, artificial grass, an old raincoat, cardboard, a tray of water, a baking tray or a chopping board.

1. Create a trail around your room or garden made out of items that your dog can stand on. If your puppy is under one year old, make sure that the items are at ground level to avoid any jumping that could damage developing joints.

2. Move a treat around the trail in your hand so that your dog follows you while walking on the balance trail.

3. Give your pup the treat when they have walked around the trail or more frequently if they need added motivation to continue to follow you.

4. If there is an item that they are hesitant to stand on, sprinkle some treats on the item, allow them to eat the treats, then move on to the next item. They may feel more confident next time you go round the trail.

5. Alternatively, place treats along the length of the trail and allow your dog to explore the trail themselves.

▲ Learning to walk on different textures and surfaces is a great sensory experience for puppies.

Human Weave Poles

Who needs Crufts-style weave poles when you have a family of humans at hand? This activity allows your dog to flex their body left and right as they weave between you, while building body awareness through avoiding bumping into you. Short of humans? Use plant pots or upside-down pans instead.

You will need:

▶ two or more willing human volunteers or a selection of large pots.

1. Have your volunteers stand in a line, spaced a stride apart.

2. Call your dog excitedly so that they follow you.

3. Keep calling them as you weave in and out of the human weave poles.

4. Give them a treat when they get to the end of the line.

5. Keep practising – in time you will be able to guide your dog to weave in and out without having to weave yourself.

▲ Weave poles allow your dog to build body awareness as they flex and stretch their muscles.

Rally Course

Rally is a dog sport where you and your dog navigate a course with signs that indicate what skill to perform at each station. It is great for running through all the tricks that you have taught your dog and can be expanded to incorporate more tricks as you train them. This activity builds communication and teamwork between you and your dog, as well as giving them some excellent physical and mental exercise.

You will need:

- ▶ eight pieces of paper
- ▶ a pen
- ▶ your dog to know at least a couple of tricks (see Chapter 5 for inspiration).

1. Number the pieces of paper from one to eight.

2. Write a different cue on each piece of paper, such as 'Sit', 'Down', 'Spin' or 'Peekaboo'. You can repeat each trick more than once if your dog knows less than eight tricks.

3. Place the pieces of paper around your house or garden, in number order.

4. Starting at number one, follow the signs, asking your dog to do each trick as you reach that piece of paper, before moving on to the next.

5. Give your dog a reward for completing each cue or, as they get more practised, at the end of the course.

Hone your trick skills and successfully complete the circuit with a personalized rally course.

Musical Bumps

Remember musical bumps from childhood parties? When the music stopped you had to get down on the floor as quickly as possible. Well, this is the doggy version! When the music stops you ask your dog to 'Down' as quickly as possible. If you want to add a competitive edge, have multiple dogs competing against each other or children competing against your dog. This activity is always a big hit in my puppy classes.

You will need:

▶ your dog to know the cue 'Down' (see Chapter 5 for how to train this)

▶ music.

1. Designate someone to be in control of the music.

2. Start playing the music. Everyone moves and dances around the room.

3. When the music controller pauses the music, cue your dog to 'Down'. Reward when they do.

4. If multiple people or dogs are playing, the slowest one down is out of the game for the next round.

5. Repeat until you find a winner or until your dog has the fastest 'Down' around.

▲ When the music stops, can your dog lie down? The fastest down wins!

Sniffari

A sniffing safari is fabulous mental enrichment for your dog. By setting up a trail with wonderful things for your dog to smell along the way, you are firing up over 100 million scent receptors in their nose (compared to the six million that we humans possess). A huge amount of their brain is dedicated to processing information about smells, so this activity will really give them something to think about.

You will need:

► six cardboard boxes – shoe boxes work well
► six things that smell interesting; ideas include a sock, lavender, seaweed, sticks, feathers, a shoe, fur, empty food containers, tea bags, a toy and mud. Get creative with what you can find lying around.

1. Pierce multiple holes in the top of each box using scissors or a skewer.
2. Place an item inside each box.
3. Arrange the boxes around your room.
4. Allow your dog to enter and to explore the sniffari.
5. Keep an eye on them as they sniff and snort their way around each box to make sure that they just smell rather than rip apart the box.
6. If your dog is an avid box chewer, keep hold of the boxes as your dog sniffs at them.
7. You can repeat the sniffari as many times as you like, adding different things to the boxes each time.

Note: If your dog is on bed rest, bring each box to them to sniff.

▲ A sniffari is a feast for the nose and a great activity for working your dog's brain.

The Fan

This is a more advanced body-awareness game where your dog has to move around and over poles of differing heights that are set in a circle, fanning out from the middle. It increases flexibility, joint movement and builds gait control.

1. Prop your first pole off the ground by placing a tin can under either end of the pole.

2. Repeat with the other three poles to form an 'X' shape.

3. Vary the height of the poles by using cans of different heights, crushing some empty cans and placing one pole directly onto the floor. The poles should be at a height that your dog can step, rather than have to jump, over.

4. Lead your dog around the fan at their own pace so that they have to step over the poles as they go. You can do this by having them on a lead or luring them with a treat.

5. Repeat a few times in each direction.

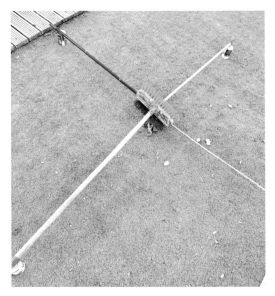

▲ Poles fan out from the middle and your dog's task is to step over them as they walk round in a circle.

Step Up

If you are looking to support your dog's hind limb strength and core stability, then this activity is for you. It's a bit like a plank exercise for dogs and all you need is something for your dog to put their front paws on. You can even put it on cue as a trick that your dog can do whenever a suitable step appears, including rocks and tree stumps when out on walks. It's a great one for capturing those perfect social media pictures of your pup.

You will need:

▶ a step suitable for your dog's height, such as a gym step, child's booster step or plank of wood supported on some books.

▲ Stepping their front feet up and holding the position will work your dog's core muscles. Put the behaviour on cue if you want to practise it in different locations.

1. Using a treat in your fingers, lure your dog up so that their front legs are on the step and their back legs are still on the ground. Make sure that they are face-on to the step rather than at an angle. Reward your dog when they have stepped up. Repeat until they are comfortable stepping up.

2. Now, start to add some duration to the time that your dog will stay on the step by pausing for a second once they are on the step before you give them the treat.

3. Over multiple repeats, add a second at a time to how long you pause with your dog on the step before they get their treat, until they can pause for five seconds.

4. Repeat several times, holding for five seconds each time.

5. You can increase the challenge by getting your dog to move their head up and down and side to side using the treat in your hand while they are stood on the step.

6. You can also add a cue to the behaviour by saying 'Step' as your dog steps up and rewarding them when they are stood on the step. This way, your dog will start doing the behaviour when you ask them to, rather than having to use a treat lure.

Watching

Although we frequently think about enriching our dog's sense of touch, taste, smell and hearing, we often skip visual stimulation. Sitting and allowing your dog to watch the world go by at the park is a great option for this; you can also tap into their desire to watch things using this simple game at home. It is a great way to introduce a little impulse control into your dog's life too.

You will need:

▶ treats, a toy or a ball.

1. Stand a little away from your dog with a treat, toy or ball in your hand.

2. Move the ball slowly backwards and forwards, up and down, as your dog tracks the item with their eyes.

3. Throw the item so that they can chase and grab it.

4. Repeat the exercise, always making sure that you are far enough away or holding the item high enough that your dog watches it with their eyes rather than following it with their nose.

5. As they get more practised, you can move the item around for longer before releasing it for them to chase.

6. At the end of the game, sprinkle some treats on the ground to allow your dog to sniff, chew and calm down after the excitement of the chase.

▲ It's easy to forget that dogs love watching and stalking prey as much as they enjoy chasing it. Adding in opportunities for your dog to watch is great enrichment, particularly for herding breeds like Border Collies.

Walk Back

Walking backwards stretches and strengthens different muscles to walking forwards, so is a great way to add a different sort of body-movement game to your repertoire. It also encourages your dog to think about how they place their back feet rather than just bringing them along for the ride.

1. Start with your dog facing you, standing on non-slip flooring.

2. Hold a treat in your hand, at your dog's nose height, right in front of your legs (the back of your hand should be touching the front of your legs).

3. Slowly, take two steps towards your dog, so that they have to take one or two steps backwards. Feel free to stop at this level if you want your dog to do the exercise without adding a cue to it.

4. To add a cue, as they walk backwards, say 'Back'.

5. Once they have taken the steps, release the treat to them. Repeat until they walk back without hesitation as you move forward.

6. Once they can consistently do this, repeat but without the treat in your hand. As they walk backwards, say 'Back'. Give them the treat from your treat pouch after they have taken the steps back.

7. Now start to move just your hands back rather than whole your body as you say the word 'Back'. Reward your dog with a treat when they have stepped back. Repeat until they can do this consistently.

8. Over multiple repeats, reduce the hand gesture that you are using, until you just have to say the word 'Back' for them to move backwards.

▲ Walking backwards works different muscles to moving forwards and encourages your dog to think about their back feet placement.

CHAPTER 4:
Baking

Baking is a fabulous family activity and a great way to get children involved in the lives of their dogs. Not only does it teach children about nutrition and looking after dogs, it allows them to show their love for their dog without any pressure on the dog to interact directly with them (see Chapter 7 for more on this). Dog treats that are bought in the shop can be full of additives and preservatives, which can affect a dog's behaviour. Making your own ensures that you know that nothing nasty is going into your dog and you know your dog will love sampling what you have made! As with any treat, the biscuits, bites and cakes in this chapter should be given in moderation. Most can be kept in an airtight container or frozen so that you can give them to your dog in small portions over days, weeks and months. Got some spare? Why not give them as gifts to your doggy friends.

Peanut Butter Training Treats

These small, easily chewed bites are my go-to for training. When training, your dog just needs a small taste of something good to keep them motivated to learn and to repay them for their hard work. Offering them a quick, tasty bite means they are soon ready for their next repeat of whatever skill you are teaching them, and that's what successful dog training comes down to – repeats and rewards. They can be stored in an airtight container for a few days or frozen to keep for longer. I make a batch of these and then freeze them, filling my treat pouch with a handful each night to give them time to defrost and be ready to use the next morning.

You will need:

▶ 150g (5oz) wholemeal flour

▶ 100g (4oz) peanut butter (nut-only peanut butter that does not contain xylitol)

▶ 1 small banana

▶ 2tbsp cold water.

1. Heat the oven to 170°C (338°F) and place a piece of baking paper on a baking sheet.

2. Mash the banana and place it in a mixing bowl.

3. Add the flour and peanut butter and mix thoroughly.

4. Add the water, 1tbsp at a time, and combine the ingredients into a dough ball using your hands. Add more flour or water as needed to get the mixture to form a firm dough.

5. Tear off a small, marble-sized piece of the dough, roll it into a ball and place it on the baking paper. Gently press down on the ball to flatten it out to a disc shape.

6. Repeat until your baking sheet is covered – the treats will not expand in the oven so can be placed close together.

7. Bake for ten minutes then leave to cool on the tray.

8. When cold, use them to reward your dog for any behaviours that you like.

▲ Small training treats such as these come in handy for learning new tricks and for when your enrichment activity calls for hard treats.

Celebration Carrot Cake

We all love to include our dogs in our family celebrations and what better way to do this than by making them their very own cake? This show-stopper is an extra special treat for an extra special pup. Try spelling your pup's name or their age out on the top of the cake using their dry food or treats when it's their birthday. You can even add pretend candles made from carrot sticks! This cake is big enough to serve it to your pup and all their doggy friends, or cut them a slice and save the rest in an airtight container in the fridge for up to a week.

You will need:

For the cake

- ▶ 200g (7oz) wholemeal flour
- ▶ 150g (5oz) grated carrot
- ▶ 75g (3oz) rolled oats
- ▶ 200g (7oz) natural yoghurt
- ▶ 1tbsp honey
- ▶ 3 eggs

For the topping

- ▶ 3tbsp cream cheese
- ▶ grated cheese for sprinkling.

1. Preheat the oven to 180°C (356°F).

2. Grease and line a 15cm (6in) cake tin.

3. Mix the flour, carrot and oats together in a bowl.

4. Whisk the yoghurt, honey and eggs together in a measuring jug.

5. Pour the wet ingredients into the dry ingredients and mix thoroughly.

6. Tip the cake mixture into the tin and level the surface.

7. Bake for forty-five minutes, until an inserted skewer comes out clean.

8. Cool in the tin for fifteen minutes, before turning out onto a wire rack to cool fully.

9. Cover the top in the cream cheese and grated cheese sprinkles.

10. Serve a slice to your pup and watch them enjoy – don't forget to sing if it's their birthday!

▲ Celebration cakes are a special treat for a very special member of the family.

Cheese Scones

Is your dog a treat connoisseur? Are they picky about their snacks? Can it be hard to motivate them to train or do puzzles? This recipe is for you. Delicious cheesy goodness that they just can't resist. I've suggested using lactose-free cheese as some dogs can be sensitive to dairy and eating cheese can result in a bad tummy. If you're going to use normal cheese, just try a small piece with your dog in advance to check that there are no adverse reactions.

You will need:

- ▶ 550g (19oz) wholemeal flour
- ▶ 170g (6oz) grated lactose-free cheese
- ▶ 2tbsp oil
- ▶ 1 egg
- ▶ 300ml (10fl oz) water.

1. Heat the oven to 220°C (428°F) and place a piece of baking paper on a baking sheet.

2. Mix the flour and cheese in a bowl.

3. Add the oil, egg and water, mix well and form into a dough ball.

4. Roll out the dough on a floured surface until it is the thickness of your little finger.

5. Cut out shapes from the dough, using any cookie cutters that you have, and place them on your baking sheet. If you are using multiple types of cookie cutter, the smaller scones will need to be removed from the oven before the larger ones.

6. Bake in the oven for about thirty minutes, until the scones are hard. Remove from the oven and allow them to cool completely on the baking sheet.

7. Store in an airtight container for up to a week or freeze some to save for longer.

8. Ask your pup, 'Who's a good dog?' If the answer is them, give them a scone.

▲ I'm yet to find a dog who doesn't like these delicious cheese scones. Great for dogs who are selective about the treats that they eat.

Ice Lollies

On sunny days, these ice lollies will help keep your dog cool and entertain them when it's too hot to go out for walks. This recipe uses apple and blueberries in the ice lollies but you can also use other dog-friendly fruit and vegetables, such as banana, mango, melon, cucumber and peas. Eating ice lollies can be a messy activity so serve in a shady spot outdoors – putting the lollies into your dog's paddling pool for them to catch before they eat will add an extra cooling challenge.

You will need:

- ► 1 apple
- ► a handful of blueberries
- ► 200ml (7fl oz) natural yoghurt
- ► 200ml (7fl oz) water
- ► 1 carrot
- ► ice lolly moulds, plastic cups or paper cups.

▲ Ice lollies are a cooling treat on a hot day and are packed with fruit and vegetables.

1. Chop up the apple, removing the core and all the seeds.

2. Blend together the chopped apple, blueberries, yoghurt and water.

3. Pour the mixture into ice lolly moulds or paper cups.

4. Chop up the carrot to make sticks that are longer than the depth of your mould.

5. Place a carrot stick upright in each mould to act as the lolly stick.

6. Place in the freezer for a few hours or overnight, until solid.

7. When ready, remove a lolly from the mould by running the mould under warm water.

8. Give the lolly to your pup to cool them down on a hot day.

Sweet Potato Pancakes

These pancakes are a healthy snack for your dog as they contain just two ingredients: sweet potato and eggs. Sweet potatoes support a healthy digestive system, as they are packed with fibre. Eggs are full of protein, fatty acids, vitamins and minerals, helping to keep your dog's coat shiny. Feed these to your dog on Pancake Day or break into small pieces as a soft treat, great for the tree snuffle (Chapter 1) and for training (Chapter 5). As an extra treat, drizzle with natural yoghurt for a gourmet dish.

You will need:

▶ 150g (5oz) sweet potato

▶ 2 eggs.

1. Peel and boil your sweet potato until soft.

2. Mash the potato using a hand blender or masher.

3. Mix together the eggs and sweet potato.

4. Heat a flat pan on a medium heat.

5. Add 1tbsp of mixture and smooth into a circle of about 1cm (½in) thick.

6. Cook until well done on one side – look out for bubbles starting to appear on the top and a brown colour underneath.

7. Flip and cook the other side.

8. Repeat with the remaining mixture.

9. Allow to cool completely and then flip them into your pup's mouth.

▲ Make sure your pup isn't left out on pancake day by making them their own sweet potato pancakes.

Banana Bites

These crunchy biscuit bites contain lots of healthy ingredients for your dog. Did you know that sunflower oil contains lots of vitamins and minerals, including vitamins E and A, which are great for keeping your dog's skin and coat healthy and glossy? They are a good option when you have some bananas in your fruit bowl that need using up.

You will need:

- ▶ 2 ripe bananas
- ▶ 2 carrots
- ▶ 200g (7oz) wholewheat flour
- ▶ 100g (4oz) rolled oats
- ▶ 50ml (2fl oz) sunflower oil
- ▶ 100ml (3fl oz) water.

▲ Your dog will love to crunch these yummy banana bites.

1. Preheat the oven to 180°C (356°F) and line a baking sheet with baking paper.

2. Mash the bananas with a fork and grate the carrots.

3. Mix together the bananas, carrots, flour, oats and oil in a bowl.

4. Slowly add the water until you form a dough.

5. Roll out the dough on a floured surface until it is about 1cm (½in) thick.

6. Use a knife to cut horizontal and vertical lines through the dough to create squares of about 5cm (2in) wide.

7. Place on the baking sheet and bake in the oven for thirty minutes.

8. Leave to cool in the oven overnight to fully dry them out.

9. Give one to your dog and place the rest in an airtight container. They can be stored for about two weeks.

Welsh Milk Chews

Himalayan yak's milk chews have become very popular in recent years. Certainly, my dogs will spend a long time chewing and eating them. Here is my take on the recipe using my local North Wales milk and Anglesey sea salt – you can personalize yours to your own area too. Chewing helps a dog settle so try giving your dog one next time they come to the pub with you or when you have visitors.

You will need:

▶ 2l (4pt) skimmed milk (semi-skimmed can be used but will produce softer chews)

▶ 65ml (2fl oz) white vinegar, lemon juice or lime juice

▶ ½ tsp salt.

▲ Chewing is a calming activity for dogs so why not take a chew with you to the café to help your dog settle while you enjoy your drink.

1. In a large pan, heat the milk until boiling, stirring continuously to avoid burning.

2. Once the milk has boiled, remove from the heat and add the white vinegar, lemon juice or lime juice.

3. Stir the milk mixture for two minutes as it starts to separate.

4. Leave to stand for ten minutes.

5. Use a slotted spoon to scoop out the curds and place them onto a clean muslin cloth or tea towel.

6. Squeeze and twist out the excess liquid from the curds.

7. While still in the cloth, place the curds on a chopping board, shape roughly into a rectangle and place something heavy on top (I use a cast-iron pan for this).

8. Leave for about four hours.

9. Remove the pressed curds from the cloth and cut into strips of your desired length: smaller for small dogs and puppies, larger for large dogs.

10. Place your strips onto a baking sheet lined with baking paper.

11. Put your oven on its low heat setting (around 65°C (149°F)) and cook for two hours.

12. Turn your oven off and leave the chews to cool inside the oven overnight. Store in an airtight container in the fridge until used. The chews will last for about a week.

★ Got a very large dog? Try doubling the recipe to make chews that are big enough for them to hold in their paws and chew.

Lick Mat Layers

A lick mat is a rubber plate covered in bumps and ridges, crafted specially for dogs. You add soft food to the top of the mat and press it into all the patterns. Your dog then licks to access their yummy treat. Lick mats are brilliant for dogs, as repetitive licking reduces activity in the sympathetic nervous system, which calms a stressed dog. I recommend using lick mats to all my clients, especially those whose dogs are receiving behavioural support for reactivity. When your pup has practised their licking, you can freeze the mat before serving to add an extra challenge. Lick mats are also great for keeping your dog happy and distracted while bathing them, clipping their nails, grooming them, when at the vets or when you have an important video call coming up! You can make a couple up in advance and keep them in the freezer for when you need them.

Scrambled Egg Lick Mat

You will need:

- ▶ a lick mat
- ▶ 1 egg.

1. Crack an egg onto your lick mat.
2. Using a fork, swirl the egg around over the top of the lick mat.
3. Cook in the microwave for one minute.
4. Allow to cool.
5. Give the lick mat to your dog – scrambling the eggs on the lick mat in this way will make your dog really work to access that yummy egg goodness.

▲ Repetitive licking helps calm the nervous system. Create your own lick mat layers with soft foods that your dog enjoys.

Other Suggested Toppings:

- ▶ natural yoghurt
- ▶ mashed bananas
- ▶ mashed blueberries
- ▶ dog-safe peanut butter
- ▶ mashed sweet potato
- ▶ mashed pumpkin
- ▶ your dog's food, if you feed soft food
- ▶ cottage cheese
- ▶ cream cheese
- ▶ pâté
- ▶ watermelon.

Pup Cup

What is better than taking a break to enjoy a coffee during your day? Enjoying one with your dog of course! Puppaccinos and pup cups have become a staple of dog-friendly coffee shops and there is no reason why your dog can't enjoy one at home too. They don't contain any caffeine and, in this recipe, I've added a few healthy extras. They are great as an occasional treat for your pup – no barista skills necessary!

You will need:

- ▶ 2tbsp vegetable or fruit purée (homemade or from a baby-food pouch)
- ▶ 1tbsp natural yoghurt
- ▶ 120ml (4fl oz) whipped cream (use dairy-free cream if your dog is sensitive to dairy)
- ▶ a sprinkle of ground cinnamon
- ▶ a small cup (I use my children's plastic ones to avoid breakages).

▲ Bring the café to your own home with a tasty pup cup for your dog.

1. Place your purée into the base of the cup.
2. Add the natural yoghurt as the next layer.
3. Squirt or spoon the whipped cream on top of the yoghurt.
4. Sprinkle with ground cinnamon.
5. Hold the pup cup out to your dog and let them lick the delicious contents.

Cinnamon Oat Cookies

Flaxseed has an array of health benefits, including being anti-inflammatory and supporting digestion, so they are a great addition to these delicious cookies. I've suggested two ways to cool these cookies to make them softer or harder, depending on what suits your dog best. The softer option is great for puppies and elderly dogs. When I bake these, I split the batch in half, leaving some soft for my senior dog and hardening the rest to be taken out on walks as recall rewards for my young dog.

These delicious cookies can be hard or soft depending on your dog's preference.

You will need:

▶ 160g (6oz) rolled oats

▶ 2 apples

▶ 2tsp ground cinnamon

▶ 1tbsp flaxseed

▶ 2tbsp honey.

1. Preheat your oven to 180°C (356°F) and line a baking sheet with baking paper.

2. Grind up half the oats in a food mixer until they have a powdery texture and place in your mixing bowl.

3. Core and grate the apples, by hand or using a food mixer.

4. Add the apples, cinnamon, flaxseed, honey and the rest of the oats to your mixing bowl and combine until you have a dough-like texture. Add extra oats if your mixture is too wet and extra honey if it is a little dry.

5. Take a piece of the dough and form into a palm-sized ball. Place the ball on the baking sheet and flatten with your hand until it is about 1cm (½in) thick. Repeat until you have used up all the dough.

6. Bake for twenty minutes.

7. For a soft, cookie texture, remove from the oven and place on a cooling rack at this point. For a harder, biscuit texture, turn off the oven but leave the cookies inside the oven for a further two hours before removing and placing on a cooling rack.

8. The cookies can be kept in an airtight container in the fridge for a couple of weeks.

CHAPTER 5:
Tricks

Training is about so much more than teaching your dog what you want them to do. It's about communication, enjoyment and strengthening the bond with your dog. Positive, reward-based training is a wonderful form of enrichment that works your dog's brain and is a lot of fun to do together (read more about this in Chapter 8). This chapter explains how to train your pup some simple, and some less simple, skills. Keep your training sessions short and frequent for the most fun for your dog and to see the best progress with new skills. One of my favourite things to do after the children are in bed is to grab some treats and, while I'm waiting for the kettle to boil, run through all the tricks that my dog knows. She loves it and it's a great way to find some calm and connect with your dog after a busy day. We always have one or two new skills we are working on alongside running through the ones she already knows, just to keep things interesting for her. Peekaboo is her long-standing favourite. Which trick will your dog love doing the most?

Sit

Sit tends to be the first cue that we teach our dogs and, although simple, Sit can be a really useful skill. Don't want your dog to jump up at you? Ask them to Sit before they get cuddles. Don't want your dog to rush out of your front door whenever you open it? Ask them to Sit before they go out. Got children who want to interact with your dog? Let them ask your dog to Sit and drop a treat for them. Once learnt, practise your Sit cue in lots of different locations and at different times of day to cement the skill.

1. Hold a treat in your fingers.

2. Place your fingers in front of your dog's nose.

3. Slowly move your fingers up and over your dog's head, so that your dog follows the treat with their nose.

4. As their nose moves up, their bottom will naturally move down.

5. The moment that their bottom touches the ground, say the word 'Sit' and release the treat to them.

6. Repeat ten times.

7. Next, remove the treat from your fingers and repeat steps 2–6.

8. Repeat until your dog rapidly places their bottom on the ground each time you lift your fingers.

9. Say 'Sit' and move your hand in an upwards motion – your fingers no longer have to be close to your dog's face.

10. When your dog puts their bottom on the ground, say 'Good' and give them a treat.

11. Repeat until your dog consistently responds to the Sit cue.

▲ 'Sit' is a useful trick as you can reward your dog for sitting rather than jumping up, running out of the front door or trying to get food off your counter tops.

Down

Here, you are teaching your dog to lie down, with their bottom and elbows touching the floor. Down is considered a standard skill to teach your pup but can actually be quite tricky. It is the skill that I have to help owners with the most in classes. This is because the exact treat placement needed to lure your dog into a Down position will vary depending on the anatomy of your dog. As a guideline, put the treat between their front paws – this works for the majority of dogs. However, if you have a dog with short legs compared to their body, or a long snout, such as a Dachshund, the treat may need to be just in front of their paws. Flat-faced breeds, such as Pugs and French Bull-dogs, find this particularly tricky because they can't easily follow the treat to the floor with their nose. For them, moving the treat from their nose slightly sideways to rest on the floor, just outside but level with their paws, tends to work best. Play around with the treat placement to find out what works for your dog and remember to reward them just for following the treat with their nose at first, so that they don't lose motivation.

▲ Training your dog to lie down is useful when you're sitting in busy areas or having guests over. Keep feeding your dog treats from time to time to help them maintain that Down position.

1. Ask your dog to Sit.

2. Take a treat between your fingers and place it in front of your dog's nose.

3. Slowly, move the treat down until it rests between your pup's front paws.

4. If their nose has followed the treat, release the treat to them. If your dog's nose does not follow the treat to the floor, move your hand more slowly.

5. Repeat five times.

6. Move the treat down between your pup's front paws as before but this time, when your hand reaches the ground, pause with the treat still in your fingers.

7. Your pup will wriggle around trying to access the treat. With their bottom still on the ground, the moment that their elbows touch the ground too, say 'Down' and release the treat to them.

8. If their bottom pops up, the treat has been placed too far away from them. Repeat step 7 but with the treat closer to their body.

Continued over

Down *(Contd.)*

9. Repeat until your dog rapidly lies down when you move the treat to the ground.

10. Next, remove the treat from your hand but repeat as before: ask them to Sit, move your fingers down from their nose to between their front paws, wait for their elbows to touch the floor, say 'Down' and give them a treat from your other hand.

11. Repeat until they consistently go into a Down position.

12. Move your hand to the ground and say 'Down'. When your dog lies down, say 'Good' and give them a treat.

13. Repeat five times.

14. Now it is time to start to reduce the hand movement needed for the skill. Continue to repeat as per step 12, but gradually reduce how close your hand is to the ground as you say 'Down'.

15. Keep going until you just have to say 'Down' or move your hand slightly down while you are still standing up for your dog to go into their Down position. Always say 'Good' and reward when they do.

Stand

Teaching your dog to stand up following a Sit or Down is useful for when they are at the vets or groomers and their tummy needs to be checked. It also allows you to give the barking burpees a go (Chapter 3), which help with building core strength for your dog. If you have a dog that you are looking to show, this skill is vital for striking a pose.

1. Start with your dog in a Sit position, facing you.

2. Place a treat in your fingers and hold the treat just in front of your dog's nose before slowly moving it backwards, away from your dog and towards you. Don't move your feet while you are doing this, just your hand.

3. As your dog moves forwards to get to the treat, they will naturally straighten their legs and stand up.

4. The moment that your dog's legs are straight, say 'Stand' and give them the treat. The aim here is that they are stationary and stood up, rather than moving a few steps forward, so don't move the treat too far away from them.

▲ 'Stand' allows a vet or groomer to work underneath your dog and is essential for dog shows.

5. Repeat until your dog stands up immediately as soon as you move your fingers back.

6. Next, repeat steps 1–5 but without a treat in your fingers, instead rewarding them with a treat from your other hand when they stand up and you say the word 'Stand'.

7. After at least ten repetitions, try moving your hand backwards as you say the word 'Stand'. Reward when your dog stands up. Repeat.

8. Finally, when your dog is in a Sit position, try just saying 'Stand' and then rewarding them if they do. If they don't, do a few more repeats of the previous step before trying again.

9. Keep practising Stand with your dog in different positions, whether that is a Down to a Stand or with them sitting next to you rather than in front of you.

Stay

Stay is a funny behaviour to teach your dog because we are actually asking them to do nothing. Stay just means hold your previous position until I give you further instructions. Here, I describe how to teach your dog a Stay from a Sit, but if your dog prefers to lie down while they wait then you can use a Down as the starting point instead. Stay is such a useful behaviour when you just need your dog to hold on a second, for instance, so that you can go through a doorway while holding cups of tea without the liquid going flying as your dog bumps through with you. You can ask them to Stay while you clean up something unsafe from the floor like broken glass or dropped grapes. With practice, Stay can allow you to open the front door for a delivery without the delivery person receiving unexpected slobbery kisses from your dog. As with all skills, it

▲ Progress your dog's Stay skills by adding more distance, walking around them and going out of sight.

is important to learn the behaviour somewhere quiet and then practise it by gradually adding more and more distractions.

1. Cue your dog to Sit or Down.

2. Hold up a flat palm up and say 'Stay', take one step away from them, then one step back towards them; say 'Good' and give them a treat. It is important that during the early stages of teaching Stay you always go back to your pup to give them the treat so that they understand that 'Stay' means don't move.

3. If your pup gets up when you move a step back, make it easier for them initially by only taking half a step back, or just pausing without movement before saying 'Good' and giving them a treat. Don't be tempted to say 'no' or 'ah-ah' if they get up before you are back to them – instead just make the next repeat easier and then move on from there.

4. Once they can consistently stay still for one step, up it to two steps, and so on.

5. Once you can move away and back without your pup getting up, start to up the difficulty level by turning away and breaking eye contact as you move away from them.

6. Next, try walking around them while they are in a Stay, rather than just away and back.

7. Finally, start moving out of sight with your pup in a Stay. Don't forget to come back to reward and release them!

Spin and Twist

Spin is where your dog starts by facing you, turns in a full circle and then ends up back facing you. Not only is Spin a fun skill, it is a good exercise to help with body awareness and balance for your dog – they have to think about what their back feet are doing! Pick a direction for your dog to turn, either clockwise or anticlockwise, and keep that consistent for your Spin cue. When they have mastered Spin, simply reverse the circle to teach them Twist. It is important to teach both Spin and Twist to ensure that the movement of your dog's muscles and joints are balanced on either side of their body.

1. Start with your pup standing up facing you. You may need to take a step back to get them to stand up before you start if they have automatically gone into a Sit.

2. Hold a treat in your hand, at your dog's nose level.

3. Slowly move your hand away from you, round in a large circle, so that as your pup follows the treat, they turn 360 degrees, starting and finishing facing you. Your feet don't move, only your dog's feet.

4. When they have completed the circle, give them the treat.

5. If your dog struggles with a full circle to begin with, start by rewarding them when they are halfway and then work up to a full circle.

6. Repeat until they can follow your hand in a full circle consistently.

7. Next, do exactly the same as steps 1–6 but without the treat in your hand.

8. Say 'Good' and give your dog a treat from your other hand when they have completed their circle and are back facing you.

9. Repeat until they follow your hand round consistently.

10. Repeat steps 7–8 but now say 'Spin' when your pup has turned halfway round the circle; say 'Good' and give them a treat when they complete the circle.

11. Repeat ten times.

12. Move to using 'Spin' as a cue by now saying 'Spin' as you begin to move your hand round in a circle.

13. Repeat, but with every repeat, gradually reduce the size of the circle that your hand is turning, still rewarding your dog when they are back facing you.

▲ Teach your dog to spin in a circle in both directions to balance the workout.

Continued over

Spin and Twist *(Contd.)*

14. With practice, you will just have to say 'Spin' and make a small turn of your finger to cue your dog to spin round in a circle. Always remember to reward them when they are back facing you.

15. Once you have mastered Spin, teach your dog to turn in the opposite direction in the same way but using the cue 'Twist'.

▲ Trick training is all about having fun with your dog and building a strong relationship.

Touch

With this cue, you are asking your dog to touch their nose to your flat open palm, like a little high five with their nose. This is one of my favourite cues because I love the feeling of my dog's feathery whiskers on my hand. Touch is a nice cue to use when you want to bring your dog's focus back to you in busy environments. It's also lots of fun because once your dog is good at Touch, you can move your hand to different places around your body and your dog will jump up or scoot through your legs to bump your hand.

---

1. Hold your hand flat and tuck a small treat between the second and third fingers of your hand, close to your palm (your dog will never eat this treat, it is just to give them something nice to smell).

2. Hold your hand down in front of your dog so that they can smell the treat.

3. When they move towards the treat and their nose touches your hand, say 'Touch' and immediately give them a treat from your other hand.

4. Repeat steps 1–3 until your dog consistently puts their nose to your hand when you offer it to them. Lift up your hand between each repeat before placing it back down near your dog again.

5. Next, remove the treat from between your fingers.

▲ Touch looks very impressive but is really easy for your dog to learn.

6. Repeat as before until your dog consistently bumps their nose to your hand when you offer them your palm, even without the treat in place. If they stop touching your hand when you remove the treat, do a few more repeats with the treat in place before moving on.

7. Finally, hold out your flat hand to your dog and say 'Touch'.

8. As soon as their nose touches your hand, say 'Good' and give them a treat.

Bow

For this trick, your pup has their bottom in the air, their back legs are straight and their front legs are bent with their elbows touching the ground – their very own downward-dog yoga pose. As well as being a fun trick, it gives them a lovely full-body stretch, helping them limber up, ready to show off the rest of their skills.

▲ Many dogs bow to stretch when they wake up. You can now put that behaviour on cue and have them bow to you any time.

1. Start with your pup standing.

2. Hold a treat in your fingers and slowly move the treat from just in front of your dog's nose to down between their front paws.

3. As they put their head down and bend their elbows to sniff the treat, release the treat to them.

4. Repeat until they bend their elbows consistently as you lower the treat.

5. Next, lower the treat to the floor as before but this time wait until your dog's elbows touch the floor before releasing the treat to your dog.

6. The moment that their elbows touch the floor (with their bottom still in the air), say 'Bow' and release the treat to them.

7. Repeat until their elbows touch the ground but their bottom stays in the air every time that you lower your hand. If your dog is lying down rather than bowing, go back to steps 1–3 and just reward for a front-leg elbow bend for a few more repeats.

8. Repeat steps 5–7 but without a treat in your hand. Instead, deliver the treat with your other hand as their elbows touch the ground and you say 'Bow'.

9. Across many repeats, you can gradually reduce the hand gesture and your dog will bow when you say the voice cue, 'Bow'.

Boomerang

Just like a boomerang, with this trick your dog will move away from you, around an item and back to you. While training the trick, use an item that you can reach over the top of, such as a plant pot, cone, bucket or pile of books. I trained my dog to do this using a stool from our breakfast bar. Once your dog is great at Boomerang, it's time to get creative and practise with a range of items, from trees to lampposts to people!

1. Start with the item right in front of you and your dog next to you.

2. With a treat in your fingers, place your hand just in front of your pup's nose.

3. Slowly, move your fingers (without moving your feet) around the item, and back to you, so that your dog follows your fingers.

4. When they get back to you, give them the treat that you were using to lure them round.

5. Repeat until they consistently follow your fingers around the item.

▲ With this skill, your dog moves away from you, around and back to you – just like a boomerang.

6. Next, repeat steps 1–5 but remove the treat from your fingers. Give them a treat from your other hand when they get back to you.

7. Repeat until they consistently follow your fingers around the item.

8. Now repeat, but when your dog gets to the furthest point away from you and starts to turn back towards you, say 'Boomerang'; then give them a treat when they get back to you.

9. Repeat at least ten times to allow your dog to associate the word with the action.

10. Next, try pointing you finger towards the item as you say 'Boomerang' and see if your dog understands what you mean and goes around the item. If they do, great work – give them a treat when they get back to you. If not, just do a few more practices of the previous step before trying again.

11. Next, it's time to add distance between yourself and the item. Take one step away, say 'Boomerang' and point towards the item. When your dog gets back to you, reward them.

12. With more repeats, gradually take more steps away from the item, repeating as in the previous step. With practice, your dog will be able to run away, around the item and back to you no matter how far away you are from it.

Peekaboo

Peekaboo is my all-time favourite trick and my dog loves it too. I know this because she frequently does this trick whether I've asked for it or not! Peekaboo is when your dog starts facing you, walks around behind you, then walks forwards between your legs and sits down facing in the same direction as you, between your legs. It's a great skill for control when something is passing close by, including people on pavements and cars on small country lanes. It can also be added to the end of your recall so that you can easily put the lead back on your dog's harness. If your dog is too tall to comfortably fit under you, then teach them to go around behind you and sit beside you instead.

1. Start with your dog in front of you, facing you.

2. Using a treat in your hand, lure your pup next to the outside of your leg, then behind your leg, then forward between your legs. You will likely need to swap the hand that the treat is in halfway through this movement – unless you're particularly good at yoga.

3. Release the treat to them when they are still between your legs and their shoulders are level with your toes.

4. Repeat about ten times, until your pup can complete this step consistently.

5. Without a treat in your hand, lure your pup next to the outside of your leg, then behind your leg, then forward between your legs. Say 'Peekaboo' as they walk forwards between your legs. Give the treat to them from your other hand when they are still between your legs and their shoulders are level with your toes.

▲ Peekaboo is my favourite of all the tricks because it builds a strong connection between you and your dog.

6. Repeat about ten times, until your pup can complete this step consistently.

7. Repeat step 5, but now slowly raise your hand upwards once your dog is in position between your legs, to encourage them to sit down. If they don't automatically sit and you have taught the 'Sit' cue, then you can use it here. Give them the treat when they are sitting between your legs and facing the same direction as you. If they walk out from between your legs and turn round to face you for the sit, then next time don't lure them so far forward before lifting your hand/asking for 'Sit'.

8. Repeat about ten times, until your pup can complete the move consistently and will sit automatically when between your legs, rather than you having to cue them.

9. Reduce the hand gesture needed for the behaviour by saying 'Peekaboo' as you move your pointed finger from just in front to just behind the leg that they loop around. Reward them when they are sitting between your legs as before.

Roll Over

Do you love an impressive trick that you can show off to your friends? Well, Roll Over is just the trick for you. Your pup starts standing up, lies down, rolls onto their back, then continues all the way over and back onto their feet. This one can take a little longer to perfect, but is worth it for the dramatic effect, especially if you use the cue 'Bang' instead!

1. Ask your dog for a Down.

2. Hold a treat in your hand in front of your pup's nose, then move it behind their head, past their ear and round and behind their back so that they have to turn their head round to reach it. Release the treat when they have followed the treat with their nose this far. Repeat ten times.

3. Repeat steps 1–2 but keep moving your hand round behind them, so that your pup has to flip onto their back to keep following the treat. Release the treat to them from your hand when they are on their back. Repeat until they do it consistently.

4. Next, repeat the previous step but rather than stopping when your dog is on their back, keep the treat moving past them so that they have to roll upright onto their paws to reach the treat. Release the treat to them when they are back on their paws. Repeat until they do this consistently.

▲ Make sure that you practise Roll Over on a soft surface to make it comfortable for your dog.

5. Then, repeat step 4 but say 'Roll Over' when they are on their back. Release the treat to them when they are back on their feet. Repeat to allow your dog to associate the word with the movement.

6. Remove the treat from your hand but repeat as in step 5, rewarding from your other hand when they complete the roll. Repeat ten times.

7. Start to use 'Roll Over' as a cue by saying it at the start of your finger movement (that is, asking your dog to roll over, with your finger just acting as a guide for the movement). Repeat ten times.

8. Over multiple repeats, reduce your hand gesture for the Roll Over, with the aim of it becoming just a roll of the finger alongside the verbal 'Roll Over' cue that will trigger your dog to roll over. Always reward when they have completed the trick.

CHAPTER 6:
How, When and Where to Use Enrichment

When to Use Enrichment

Adding enrichment to your dog's life is a good idea at any time but for more impact it can be used strategically to support contented family life. Providing different types of enrichment at different times of the day can encourage your dog to become excited and use their physical energy or can calm your dog down by using their mental energy. Both have their place in our dogs' day-to-day lives but, used in the correct order around our daily routine, can help our dogs be at the right level of arousal depending on whether it is play time or relax time. Indeed, promoting calm through mental enrichment when a dog is overexcited can ensure that they are able to settle down and nap, be calm if they are being left alone, can reduce anxiety in stressed dogs and can help avoid common behavioural problems like jumping up, leg humping and chewing furniture. Both physical and mental enrichment improve the overall wellbeing of our dogs and to understand the reason for this we have to understand the internal systems that make our dogs feel good.

▲ Providing your dog with mental enrichment can help them calm down ready for a nap.

How Enrichment Increases Wellbeing

Many hormones (chemical messengers that travel in the bloodstream) and neurotransmitters (chemical messengers that travel between nerve cells) are involved in mental wellbeing but for our purposes we're going to focus on four: dopamine, endorphins, adrenaline and cortisol. Dopamine is involved in the body's reward system and is key to motivation, focus, learning and mood. Dopamine is a predictor that good things are about to happen and, as such, are themselves rewarding, driving us to continue the activity that is going to make us feel good. The thing that dopamine is encouraging us to work towards is the release of endorphins. When endorphins are released, they reduce pain and promote pleasure. Expression of these two neurotransmitters is innately reinforcing. What that means is that activities that lead to expression of dopamine and endorphins within our dogs will make them feel good.

In contrast, adrenaline (also called epinephrine), alongside noradrenaline, is involved in flight-or-fight responses and, when released, increases heart rate and breathing, among other bodily functions. It has an effect on arousal, alertness and focus. Small amounts of adrenaline release can be beneficial but too much adrenaline leads to distress. Cortisol is a stress hormone that accompanies adrenaline in a flight-or-fight situation and is released during distress. High levels of cortisol can lead to impaired health. Reducing levels of adrenaline and cortisol and increasing levels of dopamine and endorphins will improve your dog's wellbeing.

So, what causes the release of dopamine and endorphins? For this, we need to go back to our dog's predatory motor pattern (PMP) that we discussed in the Introduction. The PMP is the full sequence of behaviours from spotting prey, through stalking and chasing, to grabbing and killing, then eating their prey during a hunt. Activities that involve seeking food, such as following scent trails, stalking, chasing and grabbing prey, cause a surge of dopamine, making your dog feel happy and excited. Activities that involve holding, dissecting and consuming food, cause the release of endorphins, leaving your dog calm and content. This is why it is so important that activities end with your dog eating the 'prey', as it calms them after the excitement. I've seen this in action with one of my own dogs, Islay, who is a Labrador Cross Golden Retriever. She loves to chase birds and squirrels and if she unsuccessfully chases them (thankfully, all but one have been unsuccessful hunts), she will come back to me with wide eyes and an overexcited demeanour. Only by scattering some food for

▲ For dogs that like to hunt, completing their PMP by providing them with food to consume will help bring their focus back to you.

her to search for and eat can I help her calm down and begin focusing on me again. In summary, if your dog is searching for food, they release dopamine, and when they are consuming that food, they release endorphins, which help reduce their levels of adrenaline and cortisol. This is why enrichment involving searching and finding food makes your dog feel so awesome.

Where to Use Enrichment

When we discuss enrichment, we often think about things to keep our dogs entertained in the house and garden. By not using enrichment when out and about with our dogs, however, we are missing a huge opportunity. Does your dog wander too far away from you when off lead? Does your pup seem to have selective hearing when it comes to recall? Is the whole world more interesting to your pup than you? For our dogs to focus on us in all environments, we need to motivate them to do so. If you are just walking along staring at your phone, listening to music or having a chat to a friend, and the only time you interact with your dog is to put them back on a lead or back in the car to go home, they will very quickly learn that coming back to you is a bad idea. Would you be motivated to get up off the sofa quickly if I asked you to come and clean the oven? How about if I said I had a freshly baked cake for you to try? For our dog to be engaged and responsive, we have to be engaging in return. Try offering your dog a piece of cheese scone (Chapter 4) every time that they come and check in with you on a walk. Recall them and then scatter feed (Chapter 1) across the grass or in a pile of leaves. Join them in hunting for a treat with the tree snuffle or play hide and seek with them (Chapter 1). See Chapter 10 for the enrichment plan to promote engagement on a walk. You are teaching them that paying attention to you and coming to you means that awesome things are going to happen, and that is how you train your dog to not go too far and to come back when called. Simple. Ending your lovely walk

▲ Enrichment outdoors keeps your dog engaged with you and more responsive to your cues.

with a trip to the pub or a café? Take a snuffle mat (Chapter 2), Welsh milk chew (Chapter 4) or egg box rolls (Chapter 2) to help them calm down and relax while you enjoy your well-earned drink.

When to Be Careful Using Enrichment

Enrichment can be used for all dogs but management is needed to keep everyone safe and happy. As enrichment is so rewarding for your dog, items such as toys and treats will be very valuable to your dog – so valuable that they may not want to share them with you or with another dog. If we put our dogs in a position where they are worried that they will lose their valuable toy or treats, they may show resource-guarding behaviour – running away with the item, growling when anyone comes near or snapping if you or another dog tries to take the item away. If you have already observed your dog showing any of these behaviours, consult a qualified behaviourist and take extra care. It is important that when you give your dog toys or treats, it is in a place where no one is going to approach them. When you give your dog toys or treats, don't try to take them off them unless you absolutely have to and only in exchange for a different toy or treat. If you have children, the dog with their enrichment should be separated from the children by a door or baby gate. If you have more than one dog, they should each be in a separate room to receive their goodies. A little forward planning with where to give your dog their enrichment will ensure that there is no conflict and everyone can enjoy in peace.

Puppies' joints are in the process of developing and hardening up until the age of around one year old (up to two years old in larger breeds). Until then, the joints are soft and vulnerable to injury. Jumping down onto solid surfaces causes an impact that can injure these delicate bones and cause lifelong damage. Therefore, when carrying out any activities that involve being off the ground, it

▲ Modify enrichment so that it doesn't involve jumping off anything while your dog is a puppy and their joints are still developing.

is imperative that puppies are not allowed to jump off. This also means that enrichment should be modified to protect their joints. For the balance trail (Chapter 3), all items should be low to the ground with no jumping off required. The treasure hunt (Chapter 1) should not involve going over any high objects. All of the adjustments are simple to implement so just being mindful of this restriction with puppies will help you protect those growing bones.

Eating food is part of many of the enrichment activities within this book, due to the release of endorphins that it triggers. However, you don't want your dogs eating anything other than food, such as pieces of fabric, cardboard and plastic. Whenever using enrichment with your dog, supervision is required 100 per cent of the time. If your pup starts to rip and swallow the toy or treat container, then it is time to remove that from

them (in exchange for a treat, of course). Whether your dog consumes as well as rips up things like the pup puzzle box or Finn's doggy bag (Chapter 2) will depend entirely on your dog. My dog, Islay, will shred but then ignore cardboard or paper, but will chew and try to swallow rope toys. If she begins to chew on her toys in this way, I simply give her some treats in exchange for the item. A good rule of thumb is to remove the treat holder as soon as your dog has finished the treats to avoid them turning their attention to eating things that they shouldn't. Whenever using enrichment, keeping an eye on your dog and making sure that they are happy and safe is always vital, and will help you reap the maximum benefit for their wellbeing.

Enrichment at Different Life Stages

Puppies

Of the behavioural problems that I see every day in dogs, ninety per cent of them have a root cause of fear. Fear in dogs can be due to lack of exposure to things in the environment or due to having had a scary experience. To help prevent our dogs developing behavioural issues, we can take action early and make positive associations with a whole range of things that they will encounter in their life. This is especially important in young puppies between the ages of three and twelve weeks who are experiencing a critical socialization period at this time, when their perceptions of things in the environment are formed and can last a lifetime. Making sure that puppies perceive everything around them as positive, whether that be noises, textures, people, scents, forms of transport or other dogs, is vital to ensuring that you have a happy, confident adult dog. If your pup is older, you can still carry out socialization, you just might need to work more slowly and support them more to create positive associations when they see something new or scary.

One way that you can create positive associations with things in the environment is by providing your pup with some fun enrichment in the presence of a range of stimuli. For instance, why not give them a pup puzzle box (Chapter 2) while playing the sound of fireworks? How about providing them with a snuffle mat (Chapter 2) when children are around? Why not park in a supermarket car park, sit in the boot of your car with your pup and give them some peanut butter training treats (Chapter 4) while watching cars drive by? Make a list of the myriad of things that your pup will encounter in their life with you and try to expose your pup to them from a distance, while pairing them with enrichment.

The enrichment itself can also be part of building your dog's confidence. The treasure hunt (Chapter 1) could take them past sights, smells and sounds in the garden that they haven't experienced before. The crunchy sock toy (Chapter 2) will expose them to loud noises while having fun. The balance trail (Chapter 3) can allow them to feel different textures underfoot and to develop their balance.

If you are getting a new puppy, make positive socialization the top of your list for your first few weeks with them. You won't get this window of opportunity back and it is the single-most important thing that you can do to avoid your dog developing behavioural problems as an adult. See Chapter 10 for the enrichment plan to promote confidence in puppies. If I could tell every puppy owner one thing it would be this: focus on socialization above all else and ensure that your puppy is happy at every step of the way by pairing their experiences of new things with something good happening.

As well as setting your puppy up for a bright future, enrichment can reduce common puppy problems. We all know that puppies love to chew and sometimes it can feel like your gorgeous bundle of fur has turned into a tiny land shark. It is completely natural for puppies to chew; it helps them explore the world and it also relieves teething pain, which peaks at about four to six months old. There is no point telling them off for this biting behaviour – it would be like me telling you off for looking at things or taking a paracetamol when you have a headache. However, you would probably also like to keep your hands and shoes intact when a puppy is around. How best to reduce the biting, then? We use two strategies: first, we provide puppies with lots of things that they can chew, and whenever they go to chew something that we don't want them to, we redirect them to their allowed chewing items. Good items for chewing include the tea towel challenge (Chapter 2), crunchy sock toy, T-shirt tug rope (Chapter 2), ice lollies and Welsh milk chew (Chapter 4). If your pup's teeth are painful, pop items in the freezer for a while before you give them to them for extra sore-gum soothing.

▲ Using enrichment to help your puppy make positive associations with things that they experience is vital to growing a happy, confident dog.

▲ Giving your puppy something to chew will stop them nibbling your fingers.

and playing games but can also be a balance trail, barking burpees, human weave poles or any of the other activities in Chapter 3. Activities such as these will increase arousal (excitement) levels in your dog, including releasing adrenaline. Have you ever arrived back from a walk or finished playing and seen your pup racing round in circles, jumping up, nipping, barking, humping your leg or grabbing things from around the house? These are all signs of over-arousal, meaning that your dog's adrenaline levels are too high and they are struggling to calm down. This is especially prevalent in adolescent dogs between the ages of about six to twenty-four months (depending on how big your dog is – in general, smaller dogs go through adolescence earlier and larger dogs later), as they are going through their challenging teenage phase. That's where mental enrichment comes to the rescue.

The second strategy revolves around the fact that puppies with an inclination to bite or chew are usually overtired puppies. Puppies need sixteen to twenty hours of sleep a day. With all the exploring, cuddling and excitement there is in a puppy's life, many puppies get far less sleep than this. Add to this the fact that puppies haven't yet learnt to calm and settle themselves, and you're heading for an over-aroused, overtired, grouchy pup and a frazzled owner. This is when we use enrichment to calm them, and activities such as scatter feeding (Chapter 1), a snuffle mat (Chapter 2) and lick mat layers (Chapter 4) are a great way to set our puppies up for nap time. We can then sit with them by their bed and give them a calm stroke as they drift off into dreams of the mayhem they will get into when they wake up.

Chewing, licking and puzzles that result in food being accessed are all calming activities for our dogs because they end with the consumption of food, which releases endorphins. Therefore, scatter feeding, the tree snuffle, muffin tin brain game, snuffle mats, pup puzzle boxes and other activities in Chapters 1 and 2 are great forms of mental enrichment. These enrichment

Adolescents

Physical enrichment is vital for our dogs as it causes the release of dopamine and endorphins. This physical exercise can be in the form of a walk

▲ Balancing physical and mental enrichment sets your dog up to be calm and settled when you have guests.

activities will reduce levels of adrenaline, which can support positive behaviour change in over-aroused dogs.

For example, if I wanted to set my dog up to be calm when I had visitors coming, I wouldn't go for a walk or play a game of fetch just before they arrived. It is easy to think that 'burning off some energy' is a good idea in this scenario but we now know that this would cause my dog to be full of dopamine and adrenaline and prepped to bark, jump up and generally be socially unacceptable when my visitors arrive. Instead, what I would do is leave enough time to do physical exercise with my dog, then mental exercise, so that they are calm and ready for a sleep just as people come bustling through the front door. See Chapter 10 for the enrichment plan for balancing energy levels in adolescents.

Seniors

As our dogs reach old age and they become less coordinated in their movements and their senses become less sharp, we see a general slowing down in both their mental and physical abilities. Using the right sort of enrichment can help maintain both muscle mass and cognitive ability, extending and improving their final years with us. Here we are looking for enrichment that includes gentle, low-impact movement and accessible challenges, depending on the abilities of your dog at that time.

Running through tricks that they already know how to do is a great option for keeping them engaged with you. The skills Spin, Twist, Touch and Down (Chapter 5) are nice options that each gently work a different body area. Scatter feeding, a tree snuffle (Chapter 1) and a sniffari (Chapter 3) are really easy options for keeping your dog active and mentally stimulated every day. A crunchy sock toy, Finn's doggy bag,

▲ Keeping our senior dogs gently challenged through enrichment helps keep them fulfilled and happy during old age.

pup puzzle box and snuffle mat (Chapter 2) are all favourites with my own golden oldie. As our dogs age, their metabolism slows down, their activity levels decrease, their appetite drops and maintaining a healthy weight becomes more of a challenge, with them easily dropping too low or becoming overweight. Using their daily food allowance but in new and exciting ways in the enrichment games just mentioned does two things: first, it makes the food more appealing for dogs who have low appetite; second, it ensures that they are not overeating and are receiving a nutritionally balanced diet. We are often too quick to rule out elderly dogs and forget that they also need mental and physical challenge to live happy and fulfilled lives. Find the right level of challenge for your dog, and you can increase their happiness and extend their years.

CHAPTER 7:
Enrichment for the Whole Family

Dogs and Children

The relationship between a child and a dog can be a magical friendship where both sides benefit. I hear many stories from adult owners about getting their first dogs when they were younger, remembering the joy and ease with which dear old Barney used to fit into their childhood lives. Rose-tinted glasses aside, creating a mutually comfortable relationship between a dog and a child takes careful management, and cues that a dog is uncomfortable are too often missed. You know those posts on social media where a child is squeezing a dog in a close hug and everyone has commented 'Aww, how cute'? Take a second look at that dog. Nine times out of ten, the dog is tense, they are turning their head away, their ears are back and you can see the whites of their eyes. These are all signs of an uncomfortable dog trying to put as much distance between themselves and the child as possible. It's easy to miss these signs when you're caught up in the moment but it's important to learn to read your dog's body language so you can recognize these subtle signs and help get them out of an uncomfortable situation when needed.

Am I saying that dogs and children shouldn't live together? Of course not – I know how much my children gain from having our dogs in their

▲ Teaching children to read dog body language helps them to form positive relationships with dogs.

lives and I know my dogs love lying with my children for story time and picking up any dropped snacks. Your role as dog guardian, and as parent, grandparent, friend or family of people with children, is to make sure that interactions are comfortable for everyone involved. This brings us back to that key ingredient that we discussed in the Introduction: choice. First, does your dog have a choice about whether to interact with the child? Second, can your child move away from the dog if they want to? Hint: the dog in that social media hug photo? They have no choice at all. This is hugely important for your dog but also for a child, so that they create positive associations with dogs without having to feel fearful or in danger of being hurt (usually accidentally, thanks to scratchy nails and tails at head height). Therefore, the key to blissful memories of childhood dogs and happy associations with children for dogs is managing interactions to ensure that everyone can have space when they want it. It makes sense when you think about it.

Keeping Everyone Happy

When I go into a home where there are children and dogs, the first thing we cover is creating a safe space. A safe space is a place where a dog can go when they need a break and they will not be disturbed. In my experience, the most effective safe spaces are places where your dog already chooses to lie down, that are out of the way of foot traffic but are close enough that they still feel that they are part of the family. You can then place their bed here, inside a crate, behind a baby gate or within a clearly defined no-go zone. You can use enrichment to teach them that this area is a great place to hang out by giving them a Welsh milk chew (Chapter 4), pup puzzle box, snuffle mat (Chapter 2) or any of the other enrichment toys and treats in this area. You may even start to shut them in

Body Language

The first piece of the puzzle when creating happy dog and child relationships is to understand when your dog is happy (and when they are not). Every dog has a different anatomy and way of expressing themselves, so your dog may not show all these signs, but take some time to observe your dog and their specific comfort and discomfort language based on the image here. When you see any of the signs of discomfort, that is your cue to help your dog have more space.

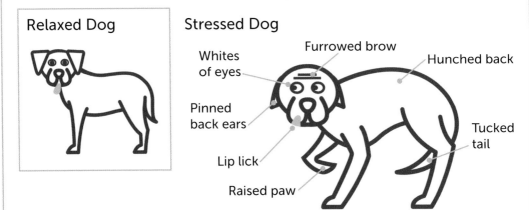

▲ Dogs use body language to communicate when they are uncomfortable. Your dog may not show all of the stress signals at once, but watch them and when they show even just one, it's time to get them out of that situation and to somewhere they feel happier.

▲ Setting up a safe space where your dog is happy to go and where nobody will disturb them is important in households with dogs and children.

this area for brief periods (start by closing the gate just for a second before you reopen it) and working up to longer periods. Always make no fuss as you put them in and let them out. Going into their safe space should be a non-event, a day-to-day occurrence, but make sure lots of good stuff happens when they are inside this space. This way, if you ever do want to shut them in their safe space, they are prepared and happy for this situation. In my house, the office is my dogs' safe space, where they have a bed and my children have been taught from a young age that this is not a room they go

into (which also makes it a great place for hiding Christmas presents). In clients' houses, we have set up safe spaces in conservatories, utility rooms and in crates in the corner of a room. The only criteria is that it is a place your dog can lie down and sleep where children can't (younger children) or won't (older children) enter.

Likewise, there are times when your children may want to be able to relax and play with toys on the floor without fear of being stood on or one of their toys being chewed. This is especially pertinent during the puppy phase when your

The Consent Test Game

Learning compassion for other living beings is a fundamental necessity for children and something that having a dog in your family can really help with, if guided in the right way. It is important for children (and adults!) to understand that dogs are individuals with their own needs and desires, and to learn how to understand what their needs are. The consent test is an easy game that you can teach to children to help assess whether a dog is happy with an interaction and whether they consent to it continuing.

▲ Pausing while stroking your dog and seeing if they come back for more is a great test to see whether your dog would like you to continue to stroke them.

1. Your dog approaches you and you start to stroke them.

2. Stop stroking them and watch what your dog does.

3. Does your dog come back towards you for more? If yes, carry on stroking them.

4. Does your dog stay where they are, look away or move away? Leave them be – they don't feel like being stroked right now.

Just pausing to check if your dog comes back for more when you are interacting with them is such a simple but effective way of giving your dog choice and the ability to opt in and out of an activity. The result? Your dog will become more confident in their interactions with you (or your children) because they know they can opt out at any time. This means that your dog is more likely to say yes to that stroke in the future.

dog is into everything and likes to chew whatever they can find. This is where baby gates become a saviour. A baby gate separating two rooms means that dog and child can both have their own space but can still see each other and be equally part of family life. Adding a baby gate is such a simple step in creating family harmony and means that both child and dog can be comfortable in their own home. It goes without saying that dogs and children should always be supervised when together; adding a baby gate gives you an easy option when you are just nipping to the loo or making a cup of tea and can't have your eye on the ball. It also means that should your dog be displaying any uncomfortable body language, you can rapidly and easily separate dog and children. I worked with a client whose dog was terrified of her young children. They created a safe space for the dog and put up a baby gate so that the children couldn't access the safe space. Within a week, the dog was no longer trembling in fear when the children were around. Don't underestimate the impact of giving your dog choice to opt out of interactions when they want to.

Enrichment for Children and Dog Interactions

Why have I included a whole chapter on dog and child interactions in a book about enrichment? Because the activities in this book are the ideal way to let your dog and child develop a strong, mutually beneficial relationship without too much pressure being placed on either of them. Let's work through some examples. Your grandchildren are coming to visit and they absolutely love your dog but your dog prefers their usually quiet life. Rather than having to say 'No, don't go near the dog' to the children (because, let's face it, when do grandparents ever like to say no to their grandchildren?), you can instead suggest that you bake some cinnamon oat cookies together (Chapter 4) and when they are cool the grandchildren can place one on the floor for your dog to come and eat: happy dog and happy children.

Perhaps it's a rainy weekend and your children are bored and starting to become troublesome. You grab some old T-shirts and help them make a T-shirt tug rope (Chapter 2) or set up a balance trail (Chapter 3). The children are kept entertained and the dog gets to have a fun game. Finally, you have friends coming over with children and you know your dog might find it a bit stressful, so you prepare some lick mat layers (Chapter 4); while the visitors are over, your dog can be in a quiet area enjoying a calming snack, learning that the presence of children doesn't have to be scary. See Chapter 10 for the enrichment plan for households with children. Allowing children to interact with dogs and learn to care for them doesn't mean they have to touch them. Children can enjoy making things that can then be given to the dog they love. This offers enrichment for both dogs and children.

Enrichment When Introducing Babies

When your dog has been used to being an only child, bringing a new human baby into the family can have a huge impact on their day-to-day life. Not only is there a new, smelly, noisy presence in the house, daily routines change and attention towards your dog unavoidably reduces. Enrichment can help you smooth the transition for your dog, by helping prepare them in advance, creating positive associations when baby arrives and keeping them entertained when you're busy.

You can start by getting your dog used to baby noises, which can be very loud for those sensitive dog ears. Play a playlist of baby noises around the house, starting quietly with the volume at its lowest, then day by day, increase the volume. While the playlist is on, provide your dog with enrichment activities so that they associate the noise of babies with feeling happy. I also find it useful to get clients who are expecting babies to start to carry things around in their arms, so that their

▲ Children can feel involved in a dog's life by making things for them without any pressure on the dog to interact with the children.

dog learns that their owner having things in their arms and walking around in circles is not something to be excited about. If your dog is jumping up to see what is in your arms, start by placing some lick mat layers (Chapter 4) on the floor near you while you practise your bouncing, baby-settling walk. The same goes for having all the equipment that babies require in the house, such as cots, pushchairs and car seats. Put them all up before the baby arrives and let your dog get used to the new surroundings, with the help of enrichment. The aim is not to get your dog really excited about these items (never put the enrichment game inside the item), but to place the enrichment in the same room, so that your dog learns these are items that they feel good around but aren't very exciting themselves.

This idea of feeling happy around, but not terribly interested in, something is a practice that

▲ Preparing enrichment in advance, so that you can give it to your dog when you have your hands full with a baby, will keep your dog happy and entertained.

we want to extend when baby arrives home too. Many people build up the idea of 'introducing the dog and the baby' and rush home after a couple of days away and immediately show the baby to the dog in peak excitement. Instead, we want to calm this right down and let the introductions flow over a few days after baby arrives. Firstly, if your dog hasn't seen their guardian/s for a couple of days, they will be really excited to be reunited with them. Make sure that your dog gets chance to say hello to you first, only bringing the baby in when things have calmed down. Next, have some calming enrichment prepped, such a tea towel challenge, egg box roll or Finn's doggy bag (Chapter 2), that you can offer to your dog as you bring the baby in and get settled in the house. Keep sniffs of the baby, and of places where the baby has been, short and sweet to begin with, moving your dog away with enrichment games (Chapter 1) and training (Chapter 5) after a short time to reinforce the idea that although babies are nice, there are more interesting things in their life.

Finally, for those times when your dog is in need of some stimulation but you have your hands full, prepare some enrichment activities in advance so that you can give them to your dog when needed. Nice options for this are scatter feeding, the muffin tin brain game (Chapter 1), snuffle mat, pup puzzle box and egg box rolls (Chapter 2). See Chapter 10 for the enrichment plan when introducing babies. These activities will not only provide your dog with mental exercise, they will leave them calmer and more ready to settle afterwards. Following these enrichment-based techniques will help you set up your family for calm, contented cohabitation and is a great foundation for helping your child form those wonderful childhood family-dog memories.

Just for Children?

Have you skimmed through this chapter because you don't know any children? Stop! Everything

▲ Learning to communicate with our dogs is an important goal for children and adults alike.

in this chapter applies to adults too. Just because we're grown up, doesn't mean that we always understand our dog's body language or manage interactions with them in the way that is most supportive of our dogs. Look at the body language guide, observe your dog, play the consent test game and learn how to tell if they are comfortable or uncomfortable in a situation. Is your dog is showing signs of discomfort? Be their advocate, help them get out of uncomfortable situations and give them choice as to whether they participate. Does it turn out your dog actually doesn't love your bear hugs and kisses? Don't worry about it; show them your love by training them to Spin (Chapter 5), playing the muffin tin brain game with them (Chapter 1) or baking them a celebration carrot cake (Chapter 4). Does someone want to stroke your dog? Check whether your dog is happy or unhappy about that idea, and if they are showing signs that they would rather just be left alone, ask the person to place a Welsh milk chew (Chapter 4) on the floor for your dog to enjoy instead. We all have the power to be more informed and supportive dog guardians, helping to make the lives of our dogs as happy as they can be in the precious time that we have with them. Enrichment is the tool that supports you to achieve this goal.

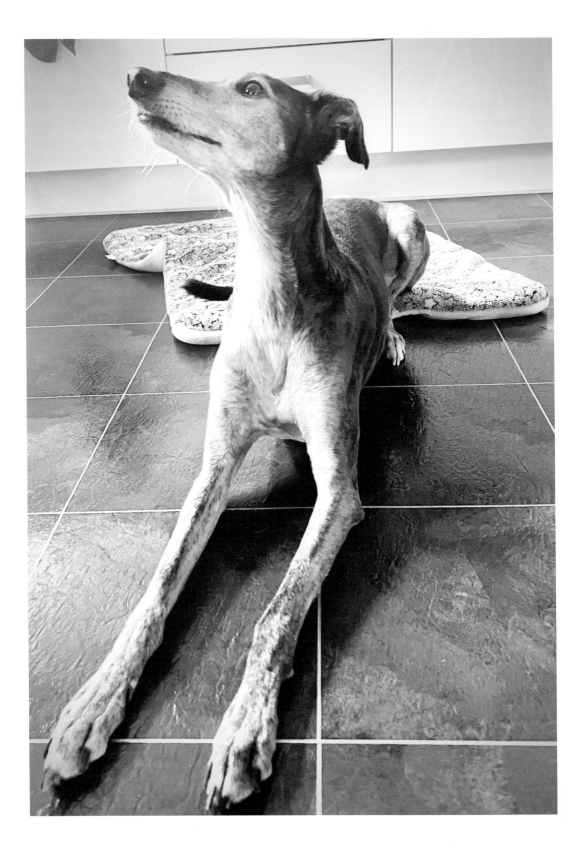

CHAPTER 8:

Dog Training as Enrichment

Why Use Training as Enrichment?

Training tricks might seem unnecessary for your dog. After all, what use do they have for doing a Spin in their day-to-day life? Training as enrichment isn't about the outcome, however; it's about the journey. Working together, communicating and rewarding your dog are key to building

▲ Training meets our dog's mental, physical and emotional needs.

a strong bond with your dog. Your dog adores spending time with you – just being with you is a huge reward for them. Giving them all your focus while you work on a new trick, or practise an old one, therefore means they are having a really great time. What's more, they are having to seriously use their brain while they pay attention and learn what you are asking them to do and how they need to move their body to get that reward. Sometimes you can almost see the cogs turning in their head as they try to figure out what is being asked of them, and when they have their eureka moment, you are right there ready to celebrate their success. Training challenges their brain, uses their body and builds emotional connection: the trifecta of great enrichment.

Positive Dog Training

Ready to work with your dog, enrich their lives and train them some cool tricks in the process? Great! However, make sure you use the right sort of training. Training your dog should be about creating positive associations and rewarding your dog as they succeed. Positive, reward-based training is about setting your dog up to be successful by breaking down the steps involved in a skill so that your dog can be rewarded for their progress as well as when they achieve the desired behaviour.

Punishing your dog for not getting something right, whether that is by saying 'no', yanking on their lead, tapping them on the nose or choking them with a slip lead is not a training experience that your dog is going to enjoy. Training then switches from being an enriching, beneficial presence in their life to being a source of concern for them, and a back step in your goal to build a strong bond with your furry family member. If I tried to teach my child to put on their socks by repeatedly telling them off when they tried but got it wrong, it would not take long before they were completely demotivated and unwilling to try any more. If you knocked over a cup of tea and someone smacked you on the back of the head, how would you feel the next time that you were drinking tea? You would likely be fearful in case you spill it and nervous around the person who did the smacking. That environment does not make for an enjoyable cup of tea. You might even stop drinking tea altogether (the horror!).

▲ It is vital that training is entirely positive and reward-based for it to be used as enrichment for our dogs.

Whether we are talking about human or dog psychology, a large volume of scientific evidence has demonstrated that reward-based learning is both efficient and effective, and not being stressed while learning sets us up to retain information long term. There is a reason that working dogs, including guide dogs for the blind, therapy dogs, sniffer dogs, search and rescue dogs, military and police dogs in the UK, are trained using positive training techniques – it is because they work! Explore what your dog finds rewarding and use that to encourage and support them as they learn new things and become your everlasting best friend.

Training Using Treats

Research has shown that food rewards are the most motivating for dogs compared with physical praise, such as a stroke, which is still rewarding but less so, and verbal praise, which they couldn't really care less about (that 'good dog' just isn't really doing it for them, I'm afraid). We have evidence that rewarding our dogs with a treat will encourage them and help them learn new skills. However, many people are understandably concerned about overfeeding their dogs, given the myriad of health problems that are linked with obesity. How, then, do we reward and motivate our dogs to do things that we like, without compromising their health?

First, a reward does not need to be a huge chunk of meat or large biscuit; it just has to be a tiny taste of the good stuff. Chop your dog's favourite reward into tiny pieces so that they just get a little piece after each repeat. Second, many dogs are motivated by their own food that you give them every morning and evening. Weigh out their portion for the day and then use as much as you like as rewards for training throughout the day. This tends to be particularly effective for puppies, who are not yet connoisseurs of a range of delicious foods, and for very food-motivated individuals, such as most Lab-

▲ Food rewards are motivating when training with your dog and allow you to repay them for a job well done.

radors. Third, think about the nutritional balance of the treats that you are giving your dog. Shop-bought treats are often packed with carbohydrates, additives and preservatives so read the label and look for the treats with the shortest list of ingredients. Making your own (see Chapter 4) ensures that you know exactly what has gone into those treats. Many dogs also like blueberries and chopped-up carrot or apple, as well as tiny bits of cooked meat. Play around and see what works for your dog, ensure that the options you offer them are healthy and try out the reward choice game (in the Introduction). Finally, ensure your dog is getting plenty of physical and mental exercise, and keep an eye on their weight through regular vet check-ups. Don't be in a rush to reduce those treats when training your dog; they are the key to long-term success and motivation for your dog, and are worth their weight in gold when your dog races back to you when you recall them across the park.

Training for Focus Around Distractions

Having an array of tricks in your training toolbox is a great way to bring your dog's focus to you when there are distracting things in the environment. Adolescent dogs in particular show low impulse control and become easily frustrated. We often see this as them pulling towards, and sometimes barking with frustration when they can't reach, passing dogs or people when on a walk. They have seen something fun and they want to get to it right now! It's good your dog likes dogs and people, but now it's time to learn some calm patience when they are around. This is where you pull out your toolbox of tricks. Take a few steps away from the dog or person and run through all the tricks that your dog knows how to do, rewarding after each one. Go and hang out in a quiet area in the park, where your dog can see but is not interacting with dogs and people, and do training with them there. The message is: yes, there are fun things around but no, you're not going to interact with them all the time; instead, we're going to do fun things together. With practice, your dog will learn that fun

▲ Trick training can help your dog focus on you even in distracting environments.

things happen with you even when other dogs and people are around, which will mean that they turn their attention to you when someone approaches, rather than racing off to intercept them.

Things You Don't Need to Worry About When Training

Finally, a word about outdated forms of training. You may have heard the idea that a structured pack, with clear dominance hierarchy, is the best way to keep your dog in line and ensure that they do your bidding; that misbehaviour should be dealt with swiftly and forcefully; or that your dog must know its place by eating after you and going through doors after you. Well, I have some good news for you. Dominance theory has been completely and repeatedly disproven in scientific literature and you can put the concept of the 'alpha dog' from your mind alongside eighties perms and the idea that a woman's place is in the home.

Way back in the 1940s, a scientist named Ru-

▲ Good dog training is about communication rather than force.

dolph Schenkel studied wolves in captivity and found that they fought for resources, and that the strongest consistently got first access to food. He called this wolf the alpha. This study went on to form the basis of understanding of wolf and dog social behaviour for the next few decades. It was only when scientist David Mech looked further at this study that he started to realize that Schenkel's study was completely flawed. The wolves in captivity had been taken from the wild, were from different packs and were all young males in an unnatural and stressful environment (zoo cages were more like concrete boxes in those days). When scientists started to study wolves in the wild, wolves were found to be in family groups comprising of a father, mother and offspring from multiple litters. The alpha and beta were Mum and Dad and the pack worked cooperatively to survive.

Not only is dominance theory not true for wolves, dogs aren't wolves! This concept was never relevant to them because they are a different species with over 10,000 years of evolution separating them from the common ancestor that they shared with wolves. How many similarities do you see between yourself and a chimpanzee? The closest thing we have to wild dogs to be able to study are street dogs, as discussed in the Introduction. Dogs show fluid social structures that adapt them to the environment that they are currently in. For your dog, this likely means a tough life of napping on the sofa, mental and physical enrichment, and cuddles. They are adapted to communicating with you so that you meet their

▲ Dogs have evolved for over 10,000 years to adapt them to their domesticated life with humans.

needs. Give them their snuffle mat before you sit down to dinner; allow them to cuddle with you on the sofa if you like; let them out of the door first if they need the toilet. Concentrate on encouraging your dog to show behaviours that you like by rewarding them for it. Use enrichment whenever and wherever is most suitable for your dog. Everything else is outdated nonsense.

CHAPTER 9:
Using Enrichment for Health

Health Check

If there's one thing that all dogs are good at, it's concealing pain and discomfort. Yes, your dog might limp and look at you with sorrowful eyes the moment they get something stuck to their paw, but with longer-term conditions, particularly osteoarthritis, skin conditions and gastrointestinal pain, the clues can be much harder to interpret. For instance, when my dog turned twelve, she started lunging, growling and snapping at passing dogs. A vet check confirmed that she had osteoarthritis and was in pain, which we are now able to manage with pain medication. The reason that she had become reactive is that she had become scared of dogs coming close to her because when they knocked into her it caused her pain. She therefore drove them away before they could hurt her. This is one of many reasons why reactive dogs should never be punished for their responses; instead we should work to understand why they are acting a certain way and address the root cause. Often, such behavioural change is the only sign that our dogs are suffering. This is why, before you start any training plan, behaviour modification or enrichment programme, a vet check is your first port of call. With the best will in the world, until we address the underlying cause of any behavioural

▲ Frequent vet checks allow you to identify and address any underlying medical issues that are causing your dog discomfort.

problems, we won't be successful in modifying them. Be mindful that pain and discomfort can be hidden and address any health problems that could be holding your dog back. Then you can move on to the fun stuff!

Enrichment and Proprioception

Proprioception, simply put, is an understanding of where all parts of your body are. It is the perception of movement and body position and is important for balance, physical exercise and avoidance of injury. You know when your dog barrels into the living room, squeezes between you and the coffee table and inadvertently knocks over your cup of tea with their back end? Well, sometimes dogs just don't know where their back limbs are and what they are doing. You may also have seen one of your dog's feet accidentally slip off the vet's table when they are stood on top of it. This is another example of lack of body awareness. Is your dog nervous or sick in the car? Lack of balance can lead to discomfort when the car moves and feelings of motion sickness. As you can see, despite it typically not being given much thought, proprioception is very important for our dogs' health and wellbeing and is a key addition to our enrichment repertoire.

▲ Proprioception exercises are important for body awareness, including balance.

Enrichment that supports body awareness includes games, tricks and activities that encourage your dog to focus on where they are putting their feet. For instance, Spin and Twist (Chapter 5) are great tricks to encourage your dog to move and bend their body while having to be mindful of their feet placement. For maximum benefit, make sure that they twist round slowly enough that their feet get chance to plant firmly on the ground as they move in a circle, rather than leap round in one jump. Likewise, for human weave poles (Chapter 3), your dog will need to think about where their body is in relation to the poles and move around them accordingly. Particularly for puppies, I love the balance trail (Chapter 3) as a way to introduce them to balancing on items of different sizes, shapes and textures. As they reach adulthood, you can also add in items of different heights. Barking burpees (Chapter 3) will strengthen those all-important core muscles and a Roll Over (Chapter 5) will add a different aspect to the way in which they feel comfortable moving. See Chapter 10 for the enrichment plan to support physical health. As always, take it at your dog's pace, find out what they enjoy and reap the benefits of un-spilled cups of tea.

Enrichment When Healing

Is your dog recovering from injury or operation and on strict bed rest or a reduced exercise plan? In this case, enrichment is all about providing mental exercise that will keep them entertained, calm and able to settle and heal. Look for enrichment that focuses on brain challenges and that will take them time to complete. Depending on where your dog is in the healing process, you may be starting with activities that require absolutely no physical movement, such as lick mat layers (put them in the freezer first to make it harder for your dog and so it takes longer for them to lick up all the goodness), Welsh milk chews (Chapter 4) and snuffle mats (Chapter 2). When

▲ Mental enrichment is key to helping a dog on bed rest to be engaged and challenged while giving them time to rest and heal.

appropriate, you can then progress to scatter feeding, the muffin tin brain game (Chapter 1), a pup puzzle box, egg box rolls and the tea towel challenge (Chapter 2). Finally, when they can move freely in the house, you can add in treasure hunts (Chapter 1), spin the bottle (Chapter 2) and sniffaris (Chapter 3). See Chapter 10 for the enrichment plan for dogs on bed rest. With a little planning you will be able to keep your dog happy and entertained while supporting their physical health and recovery.

Enrichment for Dogs Who Can't Go on Walks

Sometimes a walk just isn't the right option for your dog that day. Maybe your dog is undergoing behaviour modification for reactivity and they need time where they are not exposed to their triggers; maybe the temperature is soaring and going outside would burn their feet or leave them vulnerable to overheating; or maybe you are not physically or mentally in a place where going out is an option. Whatever the cause, there are lots of fun opportunities that we can provide for our dogs so that they can be both physically and mentally challenged in our houses and gardens. In this scenario, we are thinking about ordering our enrichment: physical enrichment, mental enrichment, nap time, repeat. Managing your dog's arousal levels throughout the day is the key to a calm dog and is especially important if you have an impatient and easily overexcited adolescent dog. Start with some physical exercise, such as a tug station (Chapter 1), digging area (Chapter 2), barking burpees, rally course or musical bumps (Chapter 3). Next, move on to some training, such as a Boomerang, Peekaboo or Roll Over (Chapter 5.) Then add in some mental exercise with a treasure hunt (Chapter 1), a tea towel challenge, spin the bottle (Chapter 2) or a sniffari (Chapter 3). On hot days, don't forget to add in an ice lolly (Chapter 4)! See Chapter 10 for the enrichment plan when staying in the house. Walks are great, but there are so many other ways to keep your dog physically and mentally stimulated without leaving the house.

▲ Through enrichment, a dog's needs can be met even without leaving the house.

Enrichment for Behavioural Problems

Reactivity

Reactivity is a stress response towards a stimulus that results in a reaction that is greater than required in relation to the threat level of the stimulus. In simple terms, your dog thinks something is really scary when in fact it will cause them no harm. This results in your dog running away, cowering, barking, lunging, growling or snapping at the seemingly innocuous trigger. Common triggers include dogs, people, cars and loud noises. When a dog sees or hears something that they perceive as scary, they release adrenaline and noradrenaline. The release of these stress hormones triggers a fight-flight-freeze-or-fiddle response within the dog. The function of these behaviours is to put distance between the dog and the threat.

Often, dogs will choose to run away from the threat, but when movement is restricted by being on a lead, by being in an enclosed space or the threat continuing to advance, a fight response will be triggered. This results in barking, lunging, growling and potentially biting the threat to make it go away before it can attack them. It may seem counterintuitive that your dog would run towards something that they are scared of but, if you like American sport analogies, the best defence is a good offence. The trouble with releasing adrenaline is that it takes hours to days to get out of your dog's system. Therefore once your dog has had a reactive response, they are primed to react again to the next thing they encounter that is a bit scary. Following the initial surge of adrenaline and noradrenaline, cortisol is released, and together this trio of stress hormones acts on bodily functions to supress non-essential systems such as digestion, reproduction, immune responses and growth. Chronically high levels of stress hormones can therefore be extremely detrimental to our dogs' health.

What can we do to reduce our dog's stress levels and empty their overflowing stress hormone cup?

▲ Enrichment activities can support behaviour modification by reducing stress hormone levels.

First, it is important that you contact a qualified behaviourist to support your dog to change their perception of triggers from negative to positive. See the Further Resources section at the back of this book for links to suitable organizations with qualified behaviourist directories. You can then support this behaviour change by reducing the level of circulating stress hormones within your dog's system through sniffing, licking and chewing activities.

When a dog uses their nose, their pulse rate lowers, and the more they sniff, the lower it becomes. Chewing and licking cause dogs to release the feel-good hormones endorphins, which reduce stress and increase mood. Adding activities to your dog's daily routine that encourage sniffing, licking and chewing are great options to support your reactive dog and reduce their stress. Furthermore, while they are engaged in these activities, they aren't hyper-focusing on the things that make them anxious. Many of the activities in this book are focused around scent work, and my favourites in the house are a treasure hunt, the cup magic trick, 'find it', the muffin tin brain game (Chapter 1) and a snuffle mat (Chapter 2). When out on a walk, I like to incorporate scatter feeding and the tree snuffle (Chapter 1), alongside letting my dog stop and sniff as many smells as they like. Most of these activities incorporate some kind of chewing too, and to really get that chewing and licking going I use the Welsh milk chews and lick mat layers (Chapter 4). See Chapter 10 for the enrichment plan to calm fearful dogs. Any behaviour modification plan that I implement with reactive dogs always includes enrichment, and now you can use it to support your dog too.

Contented Separation

Separation anxiety is based on the panic and grief emotional system – they fear that you will never come home. If your dog shows distress when you are out through pacing, panting, barking, whining or being destructive, please consult a qualified behaviourist to help you set up a desensitisation protocol. As before, generally introducing enrichment to your dog's day when you are at home will help calm their nervous system and be beneficial to their welfare. However, we can also go a step further with this by thinking about our enrichment timing.

Whether you are helping your dog learn to be content when alone or already have a dog that is happy to be home alone, the order in which you do things before you leave is important. We are often guilty of being in a rush and wanting to exercise our dogs before we go out. We march along on our favourite route or throw the ball over and over again. We then just turn round and leave. This is pretty hard for our dogs; we wind them up and then suddenly leave them with nothing to do with all that excited energy. A much better structure is first to include physical exercise, such as a walk, a movement activity from Chapter 3 or training from Chapter 5, then allow time for some mental exercise, including the games and crafts in Chapters 1 and 2; then allow ten minutes of chill-out time before you leave the house. The result? A calm, contented dog filled with endorphins and happy to drift off to sleep until their owner returns. See Chapter 10 for the enrichment plan for contented separation. Setting your dogs up for success by addressing their lifestyle as a whole is such a key piece of the puzzle in creating a harmonious and happy family life with your dog.

▲ Following physical exercise with mental exercise before leaving your dog alone will help them settle and be more content while you're away.

CHAPTER 10:
Example Enrichment Plans

To Promote Confidence in Puppies

Who it is for: Puppies, in order to happily discover the sights, sounds, smells, textures and tastes of their world.

Aim: To associate new experiences with happy feelings so that your puppy grows into a confident dog.

Overview: Exposure to novel items at your puppy's pace without them feeling overwhelmed or fearful, using low-impact physical activities.

▲ Creating positive associations with their environment is vital when raising a happy, confident puppy.

Suitable Enrichment

- Treasure hunt
- Scatter feeding
- Tree snuffle
- Muffin tin brain game
- Snuffle mat
- Digging area
- Pup puzzle box
- Crunchy sock toy
- T-shirt tug rope
- Egg box rolls
- Finn's doggy bag
- Tea towel challenge
- Balance trail
- Human weave poles
- Sniffari
- Ice lollies
- Welsh milk chews
- Lick mat layers

To Balance Energy Levels in Adolescents

Who it is for: Any dogs that become overexcited or struggle to settle down during the day. This behaviour is particularly prevalent in adolescent dogs.

Aim: To manage a dog's energy levels throughout the day so that they are able to calm down and sleep in between periods of higher-energy activity.

Overview: 1. Physical enrichment; 2. Mental enrichment; 3. Opportunity to relax; 4. Repeat the pattern throughout the day.

Suitable Physical Enrichment

- Treasure hunt
- Hide and seek
- Tug station
- Digging area
- Flirt pole
- Spin the bottle
- Barking burpees
- Human weave poles
- Rally course
- Musical bumps
- Watching
- A training session involving the tricks in Chapter 5

▲ Adolescents can become easily over-aroused but enrichment manages those energy levels and helps them settle.

Suitable Mental Enrichment

- Scatter feeding
- Muffin tin brain game
- Snuffle mat
- Pup puzzle box
- Egg box rolls
- Finn's doggy bag
- Tea towel challenge
- Sniffari
- Ice lollies
- Welsh milk chew
- Lick mat layers

For Dogs on Bed Rest

Who it is for: Dogs who have limited mobility due to injury, illness or recovery from surgery.

Aim: To provide entertainment and fulfilment with limited physical movement.

Overview: Mental enrichment activities only.

Suitable Enrichment for Dogs Who Are on Bed Rest

- Snuffle mat
- Sniffari (bring the boxes to them)
- Crunchy sock toy
- Ice lollies
- Lick mat layers
- Welsh milk chews
- Pup cup

Suitable Enrichment for Dogs Who Can Have Limited Movement

- Scatter feeding
- Muffin tin brain game
- Pup puzzle box
- Egg box rolls
- Finn's doggy bag
- Tea towel challenge (easy level)
- Touch

▲ Choosing low-impact physical enrichment will help you meet the needs of your dog even when they have restricted movement.

Suitable Enrichment for Dogs Who Can Have Low-Impact Movement

- Treasure hunt
- Cup magic trick
- T-shirt tug rope
- Tea towel challenge (medium level)
- Spin the bottle
- Sniffari
- Sit
- Stand
- Stay
- Down

To Support Physical Health

Who it is for: Dogs that are maintaining or building physical health to support body function.

Aim: To strengthen muscles, increase flexibility and avoid injury.

Overview: Slow, careful movements that focus on body awareness and core strength.

Suitable Enrichment

- Any of the movement activities in Chapter 3
- Spin and Twist
- Touch
- Bow
- Peekaboo
- Roll Over

▲ Supporting physical health through strength and conditioning is important throughout your dog's life to keep them in tip-top condition and to help them avoid injuries.

When Staying in the House

Who it is for: Dogs who are physically fit but cannot be walked that day.

Aim: To provide physical and mental enrichment to meet a dog's needs without leaving the house.

Overview: Indoor physical and mental exercise games spread throughout the day.

Suitable Enrichment

- Treasure hunt
- Scatter feeding
- Cup magic trick
- Find it
- Muffin tin brain game
- Snuffle mat
- Pup puzzle box
- Crunchy sock toy
- T-shirt tug rope
- Flirt pole
- Egg box rolls
- Finn's doggy bag
- Tea towel challenge
- Spin the bottle
- Any of the movement activities in Chapter 3
- Ice lollies
- Welsh milk chews
- Lick mat layer
- Pup cup
- Any of the tricks in Chapter 5

▲ Can't walk your dog that day? No problem! Use physical and mental enrichment activities in the house instead.

To Promote Engagement on a Walk

Who it is for: All dogs but particularly if you would like your dog to focus more on you when you are on a walk together.

Aim: To increase engagement between you and your dog when in a range of environments.

Overview: Fun activities that can be carried out anywhere and at any time.

Suitable Enrichment

- ▶ Scatter feeding
- ▶ Hide and seek
- ▶ Find it
- ▶ Tracking with tech
- ▶ Tree snuffle
- ▶ Step up
- ▶ Watching
- ▶ Any of the tricks in Chapter 5

▲ Enrichment strengthens relationships and builds engagement when you are out on walks.

For Contented Separation

Who it is for: Dogs who are about to be left alone.

Aim: To fulfil your dog's physical and mental needs and leave them calm and ready to relax in your absence.

Overview: 1. Physical exercise; 2. Mental exercise; 3. Ten-minute cool down; 4. Contented separation.

Suitable Physical Enrichment

- ► Treasure hunt
- ► Hide and seek
- ► Tug station
- ► Digging area
- ► Flirt pole
- ► Spin the bottle
- ► Barking burpees

- ► Human weave poles
- ► Rally course
- ► Musical bumps
- ► Watching
- ► A training session involving the tricks in Chapter 5

Suitable Mental Enrichment

- ► Scatter feeding
- ► Muffin tin brain game
- ► Snuffle mat
- ► Pup puzzle box
- ► Egg box rolls
- ► Finn's doggy bag
- ► Tea towel challenge
- ► Sniffari
- ► Ice lollies
- ► Welsh milk chew
- ► Lick mat layers

▲ Structuring the order in which you deliver enrichment will set your dog up to be relaxed and content when you leave.

To Calm Fearful Dogs

Who it is for: To be used alongside a behaviour modification programme for dogs that are fearful, such as dogs that react to other dogs, people, cars or loud noises with a flight, fight, freeze or fiddle response. It is also suitable for dogs who have had a one-off scary experience (such as a vet visit) to calm them afterwards.

Aim: To calm the nervous system and reduce stress.

Overview: Any activities that include chewing, licking and sniffing.

▲ Stress reduction can be promoted by providing chewing-, licking- and sniffing-based activities for your dog.

Suitable Enrichment

- ► Scatter feeding
- ► Tree snuffle
- ► Muffin tin brain game
- ► Snuffle mat
- ► Pup puzzle box
- ► Egg box rolls
- ► Finn's doggy bag
- ► Tea towel challenge
- ► Spin the bottle
- ► Sniffari
- ► Ice lollies
- ► Welsh milk chews
- ► Lick mat layers
- ► Pup cup

For Households With Children

Who it is for: Families who have both dogs and children to entertain.

Aim: To provide a way for children and dogs to be happy around each other without the pressure of direct interaction.

Overview: Activities that children can make that can then be given to the dog.

Suitable Enrichment

- Treasure hunt
- Find it
- Fastest finder
- Muffin tin brain game
- Any of the crafts in Chapter 2
- Balance trail
- Human weave poles
- Musical bumps
- Sniffari
- Any of the baking in Chapter 4

▲ Fun activities that your children can do for your dog reduce pressure on direct interactions while encouraging children to care for animals.

When Introducing Babies

Who it is for: Families who are welcoming a new baby into their home.

Aim: To create calm, positive associations with the baby for your dog and to keep your dog entertained when you have your hands full.

Overview: Easy-to-prepare activities that can be made, stored and used as needed.

Suitable Enrichment

- Scatter feeding
- Find it
- Muffin tin brain game
- Snuffle mat
- Pup puzzle box
- Egg box rolls
- Finn's doggy bag
- Tea towel challenge
- Ice lollies
- Lick mat layers (store frozen for when needed)

Final note

Thank you for delving into the pages of this book to support your dog to live a happy and fulfilled life. I hope that through the games, exercises and activities, you have strengthened and grown your relationship with your dog and had a lot of fun along the way. I always had a dual aim with this book: to help dogs live happier lives and to help guardians find pleasure in doing things with and for their dogs. This is a positive feedback loop, as the happier you are doing things with your dog, the happier your dog will be, which in turn will make you happier, which will give you more enthusiasm to do fun things with your dog. I hope you are now spiralling happily round that loop. I love to see dogs having fun so do tag me @forestsandfetch in your photos of you trying out the activities and, now that you have the knowledge, go forth and create your own enrichment activities too!

Activity Completion Tick List

CHAPTER 1: Games

Treasure hunt ☐

Scatter feeding ☐

Cup magic trick ☐

Hide and seek ☐

Find it ☐

Tree snuffle ☐

Tracking with tech ☐

Tug station ☐

Fastest finder ☐

Muffin tin brain game ☐

CHAPTER 2: Crafts

Snuffle mat ☐

Digging area ☐

Pup puzzle box ☐

Crunchy sock toy ☐

T-shirt tug rope ☐

Flirt pole ☐

Egg box rolls ☐

Finn's doggy bag ☐

Spin the bottle ☐

Tea towel challenge ☐

CHAPTER 3: Movement

Barking burpees ☐

Balance trail ☐

Human weave poles ☐

Rally course ☐

Musical bumps ☐

Sniffari ☐

The fan ☐

Step up ☐

Watching ☐

Walk back ☐

CHAPTER 4: Baking

Peanut butter training treats ☐

Celebration carrot cake ☐

Cheese scones ☐

Ice lollies ☐

Sweet potato pancakes ☐

Banana bites ☐

Welsh milk chews ☐

Lick mat layers ☐

Pup cup ☐

Cinnamon oat cookies ☐

CHAPTER 5: Tricks

Sit ☐

Down ☐

Stand ☐

Stay ☐

Spin and Twist ☐

Touch ☐

Bow ☐

Boomerang ☐

Peekaboo ☐

Roll Over ☐

Further Resources

Suggested Reading List

Bender, A., and Strong, E., *Canine Enrichment for the Real World* (Dogwise, 2019)

Chin, L., *Doggie Language* (Summersdale, 2020)

Clark, C., *Fear and Anxiety in Dogs: Understanding, Prevention and Treatment* (The Crowood Press, 2022)

Horowitz, A., *Inside of a Dog: What Dogs See, Smell, and Know* (Simon & Schuster, 2012)

Kasperowicz, D., and White, J., *Beyond the Bowl – Enriching Your Dog's Life through Food and Mental Stimulation* (Woof & Co., 2017)

Mann, S., *Easy Peasy Puppy Squeezy* (Blink Publishing, 2019)

Mueller, S., *Hunting Together!* (Independently published, 2020)

Wynne, C.D.L., *Dog Is Love: The Science of Why and How Your Dog Loves You* (Quercus, 2019)

Qualified Trainers and Behaviourists

Animal Behaviour and Training Council: https://abtc.org.uk/

Association of Pet Behaviour Counsellors: https://www.apbc.org.uk/find-an-apbc-member/

Association of Pet Dog Trainers: https://apdt.co.uk/

Certified Clinical Animal Behaviourists: https://www.ccab.uk/practising-ccabs

Institute of Modern Dog Trainers and Behaviour: https://www.imdt.uk.com/find-a-qualified-imdt-trainer

Bibliography

Introduction

Bender, A., and Strong, E., Canine Enrichment for the Real World (Dogwise, 2019)

Coppinger, R., and Coppinger, L., Dogs: *A Startling New Understanding of Canine Origin, Behavior, and Evolution* (University of Chicago Press, 2001)

Fernandez, E.J., and Martin, A.L., '*Animal Training, Environmental Enrichment, and Animal Welfare: A History of Behavior Analysis in Zoos*', Journal of Zoological and Botanical Gardens 2 (2021, pp.531–543)

Wagman, J.D., Lukas, K.E., Dennis, P.M., Willis, M.A., Carroscia, J., Gindlesperger, C., and Schook, M.W., '*A Work-for-Food Enrichment Program Increases Exploration and Decreases Stereotypies in Four Species of Bears*', Zoo Biology 37 (2018, pp.3–15)

Wynne, C.D.L., *Dog Is Love: The Science of Why and How Your Dog Loves You* (Quercus, 2019)

Chapter 6

Asher, L., England, G.C.W., Sommerville, R., and Harvey, N.D., '*Teenage Dogs? Evidence for Adolescent-Phase Conflict Behaviour and an Association between Attachment to Humans and Pubertal Timing in the Domestic Dog*', Biology Letters 16, (2020, pp.1–5)

Barrett, L.F., *How Emotions Are Made* (Pan, 2018)

Dietz, L., Arnold, A.M.K., Goerlich-Jansson, V.C., and Vinke, C.M., '*The Importance of Early Life Experiences for the Development of Behavioural Disorders in Domestic Dogs*', Behaviour 155 (2018, pp.83–114)

Horowitz, A., *Inside of a Dog: What Dogs See, Smell, and Know* (Simon & Schuster, 2012)

Hunt, R.L., Whiteside, H., and Prankel, S., '*Effects of Environmental Enrichment on Dog Behaviour: Pilot Study*', Animals 12 (2022, pp. 1 8)

Lefebvre, D., Giffroy, J.M., and Diederich, C., '*Cortisol and Behavioral Responses to Enrichment in Military Working Dogs*', Journal of Ethology 27 (2009, pp.255–265)

Moberg, G., and Mench, J. (eds), *The Biology of Animal Stress* (CABI Publishing, 2000)

Sapolsky, R.M., *Behave* (Vintage, 2018)

Schipper, L.L., Vinke, C.M., Schilder, M.B.H., and Spruijt, B.M., *The Effect of Feeding Enrichment Toys on the Behaviour of Kennelled Dogs (Canis familiaris)'*, Applied Animal Behaviour Science 114 (2008, pp.182–195)

Chapter 7

Aloff, B., *Canine Body Language: A Photographic Guide* (Dogwise, 2005)

Chin, L., *Doggie Language* (Summersdale, 2020)

Chapter 8

China, L., Mills, D.S., and Cooper, J.J., *'Efficacy of Dog Training with and without Remote Electronic Collars vs. a Focus on Positive Reinforcement'*, Frontiers in Veterinary Science 7, (2020, pp.1–3)

de Castro, A.C.V., Fuchs, D., Morello, G.M., Pastur, S., de Sousa, L., and Olsson, I.A.S., *'Does Training Method Matter? Evidence for the Negative Impact of Aversive-Based Methods on Companion Dog Welfare'*, PLoS ONE 15 (2020, pp.1–26)

Dinwoodie, I.R., Zottola, V., and Dodman, N.H., *'An Investigation into the Impact of Pre-Adolescent Training on Canine Behavior'*, Animals 11 (2021, p.1298)

Hedges, S., *'Unravelling Dominance in Dogs'*, The Veterinary Nurse 8 (2017, pp.132–138)

Herron, M.E., Shofer, F.S., and Reisner, I.R., *'Survey of the Use and Outcome of Confrontational and Non-Confrontational Training Methods in Client-Owned Dogs Showing Undesired Behaviors'*, Applied Animal Behaviour Science 117 (2009, pp.47–54)

Mech, L.D., *'Leadership in Wolf, Canis lupus, Packs'*, Canadian Field Naturalist 114 (2000, pp.259–263)

Pryor, K., *Don't Shoot the Dog! The Art of Teaching and Training* (Simon & Schuster, 2019)

Chapter 9

Carter, L., *The Vet Says Rest* (Independently published, 2023)

Clark, C., *Fear and Anxiety in Dogs: Understanding, Prevention and Treatment* (The Crowood Press, 2022)

Duranton, C., and Horowitz, A., *'Let Me sniff! Nosework Induces Positive Judgment Bias in Pet Dogs'*, Applied Animal Behaviour Science 211 (2019, pp.61–66)

Herron, M.E., Kirby-Madden, T.M., and Lord, L.K., *'Effects of Environmental Enrichment on the Behavior of Shelter Dogs'*, Journal of the American Veterinary Medical Association 244 (2014, pp.687–692)

Mills, D.S., Demontigny-Bédard, I., Gruen, M., Klinck, M.P., McPeake, K.J., Barcelos, A.M., Hewison, L., Van Haevermaet, H., Denenberg, S., Hauser, H., Koch, C., Ballantyne, K., Wilson, C., Mathkari, C.V., Pounder, J., Garcia, E., Darder, P., Fatjó, J., and Levine, E., *'Pain and Problem Behavior in Cats and Dogs'*, Animals 10 (2020, pp.1–20)

Index

First published in 2024 by
The Crowood Press Ltd
Ramsbury, Marlborough
Wiltshire SN8 2HR

enquiries@crowood.com

www.crowood.com

British Library Cataloguing-in-
Publication Data
A catalogue record for this book is available
from the British Library.

ISBN 978 0 7198 4399 0

Cover design by Su Richards

Typeset by Su Richards
Printed in India by Parksons Graphics

Acknowledgements

Huge thanks to my husband, Martin,
who has made time for me to write this
book, has listened to my ideas for content, taken photos and created beautiful
graphics. As with everything I do, he
should probably be a co-author. I am
very grateful to my sons, Finn and Bro-
die, who have provided endless enthusiasm for creating, trialling and improving
the activities in this book. Seeing the
joy that they get from making our dogs
happy inspired me to write this family-friendly book. Thanks to my parents
for proofreading my draft and providing
inspiration for the grandparents who like
to say yes. To my trio of wonderful dogs,
Skye, Islay and Bella, you have provided
the perfect testers in the senior, adult and
puppy categories and I hope that the fun
that you get from these activities goes in
some way to thanking you for all the joy
that you give me.

The gorgeous dogs in this book have
all worked with me for training and
behaviour support. Thank you to their
owners for choosing me to support their
training journey and allowing me to
take and use these photos of their dogs.
Thanks to the dogs for posing so beau-
tifully and making my job so enjoyable.
Thanks also to the human models in the
photos who graciously gave their time
and energy. I hope you enjoy doing the
enrichment activities in the book!

Finally, thanks to The Crowood Press
for giving me the opportunity to write
about something that I am passionate
about and supporting me in that journey.
What a pleasure it has been.

Related Titles from Crowood

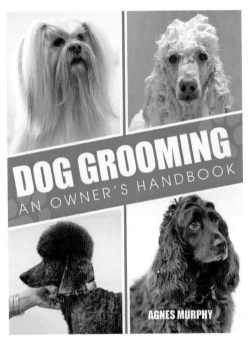

ISBN: 978 0 71984 307 5

ISBN: 978 0 71984 183 5

ISBN: 978 0 71984 112 5

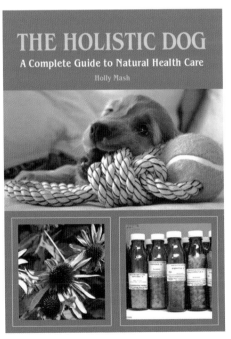

ISBN: 978 1 84797 267 5